TO:

FROM:

**Since this book is for families, I wanted to include mine.
Here is what family means to them:**

"Family is love, hugs, and warm fuzzies."

JANICE EMERZIAN

Mom

"Family means loving, supporting, caring,
and sharing life's moments together."

RON EMERZIAN

Dad

"Family is pizza on Christmas Eve, camping at the
beach, and playing cards with my in-laws."

PATTY MALCOLM EMERZIAN

Wife

"Family means everything."

KATHLEEN MALCOLM

Mother-in-law

"Family is forever."

VICTOR MALCOLM

Late father-in-law

"Family are those who create us, who shape us, and for whom we try to be our best selves, so we can do the same for those we love and who come after us."

MICHAEL EMERZIAN

Brother

"Family are those who stand by you, walk with you, and play game nights."

MELISSA EMERZIAN

Sister-in-law

"A family is a community that loves one another so deeply despite personal flaws. The love shared is eternal and offers support and compassion."

GAVIN EMERZIAN

Nephew

"Family doesn't have to come down to genetics. It means to be around those who support and accept you for who you are. They love you unconditionally and will be there for you no matter what."

KATE EMERZIAN

Niece

"Family nourishes your heart and nurtures your soul."

JOHN MATOIAN

Uncle

"Family is a bond like no other."

MATTY MATOIAN

Uncle

"If you always remember those who shaped
you, they will never leave you."

BARBARA BOGART

Aunt

"My family gives me the path to follow. It is the foundation
of who I am and what I strive to be every day."

CHAD MATOIAN

First cousin

"Family is that our three daughters love us so deeply
and with no judgments or expectations other than
that we love them back in the exact same way."

BRADY MATOIAN

First cousin

"Family is shelter from the storms."

GEOFF BOGART

First cousin

"Family is a crowded table. A place of belonging,
security, support, acceptance, and inclusion."

DANA WRONSKI

First cousin

"My family is my life, and everything
else comes second to me."

DIANE MALCOLM

Sister-in-law

"Families are like fudge…mostly sweet with a few nuts."

STEVE MALCOLM

Brother in-law

EVERY MONDAY MATTERS

FOR FAMILIES

52 WEEKS TO MAKE A POSITIVE DIFFERENCE FOR YOU, YOUR FAMILY, AND YOUR COMMUNITY

MATTHEW EMERZIAN

Published by Simple Truths, an imprint of Sourcebooks
P.O. Box 4410, Naperville, Illinois 60567-4410
(630) 961-3900
sourcebooks.com

Printed and bound in China
OGP 10 9 8 7 6 5 4 3 2 1

For every single person who has played a role, no matter how big or small, in the Every Monday Matters story. You will always be a part of our family. You matter.

CONTENTS

PREFACE: MY STORY   xii

INTRODUCTION   xiv

MONDAY GETS FUN

Get Goofy   2

Lend a Hand   4

Surprise Someone   6

Spice It Up   8

MONDAY GETS ACCEPTING

Embrace Uniqueness   12

Celebrate Change   14

Know What Matters Most   16

Ask for Input   18

MONDAY GETS CONSISTENT

Be Patient   22

Put in the Work   24

Believe in Boundaries   26

Honor Your Word   28

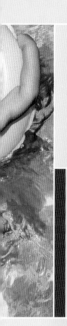

MONDAY GETS HEALTHY

Take Ownership	32
Practice Peace	34
Check Your Choices	36
Feel the Feels	38

MONDAY GETS LOVING

Ask Questions	42
Make Time	44
Curate Compassion	46
Choose Kindness	48

MONDAY GETS MINDFUL

Enjoy the Now	52
Be Intentional	54
Unplug to Plug In	56
Simplify Your Life	58

MONDAY GETS CONNECTED

Make a Memory	62
Open the Door	64
Value Tradition	66
Go with Grace	68

MONDAY GETS SPECTACULAR

Feel the Wonder 72

Own Your Awesomeness 74

Prepare to Launch 76

Go Big 78

MONDAY GETS ADVENTUROUS

Conquer a Fear 82

Decide to Discover 84

Change Your Routine 86

Start a Hobby 88

MONDAY GETS COMPASSIONATE

Walk in Their Shoes 92

Right a Wrong 94

Build Bridges 96

Listen Up 98

MONDAY GETS GRATEFUL

Give Gratitude 102

Love the Little Things 104

Give One, Give One 106

Waver No More 108

MONDAY GETS EMPOWERED

Connect to Purpose 112

Be Tenacious 114

Get Back Up 116

Celebrate the Effort 118

MONDAY GETS HOPEFUL

Light Up the Room 122

Practice Positivity 124

Start a Legacy 126

Believe It's Possible 128

FAMILY DINNER CONVERSATION STARTERS

130

ABOUT THE AUTHOR

140

PREFACE: MY STORY

Fifteen years ago, I started a journey. I didn't necessarily have a plan, but I had a deep desire to help people know how much they mattered. I had just come out the other side of a very dark time in my life, crippled by anxiety and depression, and I simply didn't want anyone to ever experience such pain. Easier said than done, I know, but something told me I could help people and our world.

I was one of the lucky ones. I had resources and a family who loved and supported me. I was able to get the proper help, which allowed me to find new meaning and purpose in life. It took time and a lot of hard work, but today, I can actually say that I am a better person because of my brokenness. My breakdown was the biggest blessing…not just for me but for millions of people.

In 2007, I wrote the first Every Monday Matters book with a friend of mine. That book became the catalyst for a nonprofit organization that I founded, aptly called Every Monday Matters. Our mission is to create a world where everyone knows how much and why they matter. We currently serve over two million students with our K-12 curriculum; we help companies create cultures where their employees feel like they matter at work; and I get the great pleasure of doing keynotes and writing books to reach more individuals like you with our message.

It is hard to believe that this is the fourth book I have written and that you are now holding it in your hands. I hope this book brings you and your family great joy and a new sense of purpose. I hope it connects you in new and more significant ways. And I hope it helps you embrace how much you matter to yourself, your family, and your community.

As a last note, you should know I don't receive a single penny from your purchase of this book; rather your hard-earned money is going to support our education program so we can reach more youth. See, you have already made a difference.

Thanks so much. As I told you, "You matter."

INTRODUCTION

With every new day, it has become clearer to me that we were designed to live life in relationship with others. I know there are introverts and extroverts and that some of us might thrive more in social settings than others, but that doesn't alter my conviction. Even the most introverted, shyest, quietest person in the world needs connection and community.

Unfortunately, however, we have found ourselves on the fast track to disconnection and isolation, and there are a lot of forces driving that train: We are living at a pace far too fast to be present and to enjoy the moment. We have fooled ourselves into believing that our connections with followers or friends on social media are actually rich, life-giving relationships. We can order anything online and have it delivered to our doors without ever seeing a single person. We are divided more than ever, socially and politically, and it is tearing us apart, including families. And to make matters worse, we have been in the throes of a virus that has kept us cocooned away from one another. Oh, how I miss seeing smiles, which have been covered by masks for months.

The combination of the above doesn't just bother me; it is actually not healthy for any of us. Research now suggests that isolation and loneliness are greater health risks than heart disease. It's time for us to take note and to take action, and this book is a recipe for that. Because there is a force that is more powerful than all this; it's called *family*, and it is everything to our existence. I believe that reinvesting in the concept of the family unit is exactly what we need, both individually and collectively. This is why I am so excited about this book. I believe it is going to change everything.

Let me be clear from the get-go about what I mean by the term *family*, because I understand this is not a one-size-fits-all concept. In fact, I believe we are all part of several families throughout our journeys. Our biological or adopted families are the most obvious choice, but our neighborhoods are families. Our colleagues at work are our families. Same with any teams we are part of, clubs, classrooms, associations, friendships, and even the world. All these are "we" things. So let's consider a family any occasion when two or more people come together and exist in relationship with one another over a period of time.

It will also help to share that this book is not just a book that you *read* but one that you *do*. It is one thing to hear that you matter, but it is something entirely more profound to experience it. To make it easier, the book is broken down into thirteen chapters. Each chapter has a theme—adventurousness, compassion, acceptance, empowerment, etc. Then, each chapter includes four Mondays, weekly strategies to help you and your family experience the significance of each monthly theme.

As you will discover, each Monday offers a mindful moment for you and your family to read and process together, then it provides several opportunities for you to engage. First, there are three engagement options for each week: **FOR YOU**, **FOR YOUR FAMILY**, and **FOR YOUR COMMUNITY**. These are all about you taking action. Second, the back of the book offers a **FAMILY DINNER CONVERSATION STARTER** section to help you and your family engage in meaningful conversations that help you grow, both individually and as a unit.

The last thing I want to share before I step aside so you and your family can begin this incredible journey is that you might notice that throughout the book, I use the pronoun "we" instead of "I." I did this because even though my name is on the front of this book, it certainly wasn't all done by me. Because this book is for families, I intentionally included several people in this process. These are Every Monday Matters team members, like Jocelyn and our amazing education team. These are families of all different compositions and from all different places around the country. And these are some of my friends and family members whom I cherish dearly. So this book is from our family to yours. It is a "we" thing through and through, which only makes it that much more special to me.

Enjoy your journey. And please email me and share your stories. Your stories will inspire more inspiring stories, and that is what life is all about. You matter. Your family matters.

MATTHEW EMERZIAN
matthew@everymondaymatters.com

MONDAY GETS FUN

When did everything get so serious? Seriously. Sure, we get it. We all have responsibilities—there's homework to do, deadlines to meet, errands to run, chores to finish, bills to pay, exercise to get in. But we can't let all this keep us from enjoying life. We're allowed to have a little bit of fun. So we have two options to consider, and frankly, we think they are both good ones. First, we can switch up our mindsets and choose to find more fun in our responsibilities. Instead of thinking, "Ugh, I need to go to the gym," how about saying, "I love going for a run because I get to be outside, see people and nature, and feel great when I'm finished"? See, exercise just got a whole lot more appealing. The second option is about carving out space for adding new and fun experiences to your life. Think you and your family can find a few extra minutes for something fun? Are you already smiling just thinking about it? That's how powerful and important having fun truly is. Fun matters.

THIS WEEK...
GET GOOFY

There's a question we used to ask on a regular basis. It's not that "Why?" question we threw at our parents or guardians or that your children throw at you now. Isn't life cruel that way? It's the "Can you play today?" question. Sound familiar? Our guess is that you might have heard your children ask this question of their friends a few times but you have not uttered those words in quite a while. Well, that's all about to change, because this week, we want you to **GET GOOFY**. Yes, we are asking if you can play today. When is the last time you let loose and played a fun game with your family? What game was it, and why was it so fun? When is the last time you threw a family dance party or played charades? The options are endless, as long as you are willing to get goofy with it. Just let your children pick the game or activity if it helps. They will have you laughing in no time. Whatever you end up doing, have a blast playing and connecting with one another. You can even go one step further and offer participation trophies for making the time to play with you this week. However you go about it, we're happy to know you are getting wacky and playing games, being creative, and having fun together. Getting goofy matters.

REMEMBER TO PLAY AFTER EVERY STORM.

— Mattie Stepanek

TAKE ACTION

FOR YOUR COMMUNITY: Host a community goofy challenge. Maybe it is a sidewalk chalk drawing competition. Maybe it is a neighborhood talent show. Or maybe it is a street carnival, and every family is responsible for a goofy station. Organize it…then have a blast.

FOR YOUR FAMILY: Family game nights are a must for every family. Put them on the calendar, and never miss one. Each game night, ask one another, "Can you play today?" Then plan something fun together and play. Doesn't get any easier than this.

FOR YOU: Spend some time thinking about the games you used to like to play the most, the games you currently enjoy, or maybe some that you have never played before but you would like to. Pickleball, anyone? Pick one and go play. Just promise to smile and laugh a lot.

THIS WEEK...
LEND A HAND

TAKE ACTION

FOR YOUR COMMUNITY: As a family, write out a bunch of sweet and uplifting sayings on Post-it notes. The more the merrier. Then take them out into your community, and stick them in random places for people to enjoy. Congratulations on bringing smiles to your community.

FOR YOUR FAMILY: Do a fun family project where everyone can lend a hand. Maybe it is something that already exists, like a local escape room. Or maybe you put together a play and invite friends, neighbors, and other family members to enjoy. Just make sure everyone can lend their hand.

FOR YOU: Are you good at asking for and receiving help? If not, instead of seeing it as weakness or something negative, see it as a fun opportunity to do life together with someone. If you focus on being appreciative and having fun, you'll never want to fly solo again.

> **THE PURPOSE OF HUMAN LIFE IS TO SERVE, AND TO SHOW COMPASSION AND THE WILL TO HELP OTHERS.**
>
> —Albert Schweitzer

Recall for a moment the last time you entered a store and an employee asked if they could help you. Do you remember how you replied? Did it sound something like, "Oh, no, thank you. I am just looking"? All they were doing was offering to help. Maybe you looked a little lost or confused—and maybe you were—but all you wanted to do was shut down the gesture as quickly as possible. The bummer part of this is that serving others and helping one another is actually a lot of fun. We are wired for it. When we are in service, we are at our very best. So this week, we want you to **LEND A HAND**. This might feel like a setup, since we just established that we don't like receiving help, but sometimes we need to push one another to grow. In this case, we can help one another find the fun and joy in giving and receiving help. When we lend a hand, we show interest in someone. When we lend a hand, we learn new things. When we lend a hand, we share meaningful experiences together. So be on the lookout for opportunities to jump in and serve someone in your family. Maybe it is a project at work or school or something around the house. The key is taking action and stepping in. Lending a hand matters.

SURPRISE SOMEONE

Typically, surprises are saved for birthdays and April Fools' Day, so at the most, you might be able to surprise the same person twice in one year. But surprises, when done in a kind, loving, and fun way, are absolute happiness machines. Sure, there is a little shock in the beginning, but that eyes-wide-open, hands-over-the-mouth look quickly turns into smiling and laughter. There is nothing wrong with more smiling and laughter in our lives, so this week, we want you to **SURPRISE SOMEONE**. Now here is the thing: please be thoughtful and respectful with your surprise idea. This isn't the rubber snake in the drawer sort of surprise. This is the type that surprises someone both because it is unexpected and because it is meaningful. And know that it doesn't need to be a big hoopla. A meaningful letter or a simple flower will do the trick. Preparing someone's favorite dinner, just because, is a great surprise. Then again, throwing a birthday party for your spouse when it's not even their birthday is pretty cool as well. You get the idea here. Let's make it fun. Let's make it meaningful. The effort alone is what makes it special. Surprising someone matters.

TAKE ACTION

FOR YOUR COMMUNITY: Throw a free car wash for your community. Gather your team and supplies, pick your day, time, and location, put up signs to promote it, and wash away. Remember, though, this is a free car wash, which will only add to the fun and awesomeness of the surprise.

FOR YOUR FAMILY: You have two super fun options this week. Either throw a surprise party for your family, which means they can't have read this, or as a family, throw a surprise party for another family. Remember, you don't need a reason. "Just for the love of fun" is more than enough.

FOR YOU: Treat yourself to something. It's that thing you have always wanted to do or buy but instead settled with "Oh, I just can't do that." Well, do it. You have full permission now.

IN MOMENTS OF SURPRISE, WE CATCH AT LEAST A GLIMPSE OF THE JOY TO WHICH GRATEFULNESS OPENS THE DOOR.

—David Steindl-Rast

7

THIS WEEK...
SPICE IT UP

TAKE ACTION

FOR YOUR COMMUNITY: Find a community events calendar—most likely you can celebrate Oktoberfest, Carnival, and the tulip festival right in your home-town. Find a local pub that shows international soccer or rugby games, and go root for the pub's favorite team.

FOR YOUR FAMILY: It's international family dinner week. Every night is a new food from a new country. Get everyone involved. Throw on some corresponding international music, and spice it up together.

FOR YOU: If you could visit a new country right this minute, where would you go? Why? Write a magazine article or blog about it, and share it with your family. Get everyone to fall in love with it. And maybe, just maybe, one day, you can all go there together.

> I JUST THINK YOU NEED TO SPICE UP LIFE EVERY NOW AND THEN WITH A BIT OF ADVENTURE AND EXCITEMENT.

—Richard Branson

People are the spice of life. Fortunately, we live in a world today where we are surrounded by beautiful and unique cultures. We might have neighbors, colleagues, classmates, and even family members who come from very different cultures than our own. Have you ever taken a moment to realize how fun this is? Literally, we can travel the world without having to ever jump on a plane. So let's take that world tour. This week, we want you to **SPICE IT UP**. Cultures are made up of different beliefs and values, different traditions and languages, different foods and art. Learning about these different cultures not only helps us grow individually, it is the catalyst for creating a more compassionate and caring world. Last time we checked, food and music make for some pretty fun moments in life. So get ready to expose your taste buds to some new flavors. Get ready to treat your ears to some new sounds. There is a great big world out there, just around the corner from your family, waiting for you enjoy it. Have fun. Be curious. Enjoy the beautiful mosaic of humanity. Spicing it up matters.

MONDAY GETS ACCEPTING

Although we all may be part of the same family, it doesn't mean we are all the same. Nor does it mean we should all strive to be the same. Families are simply collections or groupings of individuals. Yes, even if we share the same last name, we are still individuals coming together to create the whole. This is a beautiful concept, for it's how the most beautiful mosaics and stained glass windows are created. However, this can be challenging, as it requires us to honor and celebrate one another, even when we don't see eye to eye. It begs us to appreciate the fact that two people can see the same thing very differently. Note, this does not mean we can condone blank checks for falsehoods. We have to establish some set of standards, a moral compass, or a universal truth that establishes right from wrong, fact from fiction, and that there is a right way to live. From that baseline, we can then begin to not just tolerate one another but actually appreciate everyone's uniqueness. So let's celebrate what each member brings to the family. Let's truly value what it means to be a family. Being accepting matters.

EMBRACE UNIQUENESS

We spend so much of our lives trying to fit in. Maybe we wanted to be one of the "cool kids." Maybe we were worried what people would think about the color of our skin, our jumbo reading glasses, or our big ears. Or maybe we were fearful of being judged because we couldn't afford new school clothes or a new backpack every first day of school. Being called out for our differences instantly made us feel less than, unworthy, and unaccepted. Heartbreakingly, this continues into adulthood, creating a culture of social disparity and injustice. But what would our world and our families look like if we simply **EMBRACE UNIQUENESS**? Behind the eyes of every human being is a heart, a soul, and a story. Each one of these stories is littered with fear, insecurity, joy, celebration, heartache, hope, love, rejection, and a deep desire to feel like we matter to someone or something. These stories are what we have in common, although they are all beautifully and tragically unique. Let's ask and listen. Let's honor the stories. Embracing uniqueness matters.

TAKE ACTION

FOR YOUR COMMUNITY: Think of five people in your life, then think about one thing that makes each of them unique. Take time this week to make sure they know how much you appreciate them for their unique gift, trait, or talent. After all, isn't "unique" a sweeter way of saying "different"?

FOR YOUR FAMILY: Create a "Get to Know You Better" interview event. Have each family member write three questions they would like to ask each member of the family. Then start the interviews. Rotate interviewees until everyone has been interviewed. Be kind. This is about acceptance, not a roast.

FOR YOU: Has there ever been a time when you felt like you didn't fit in or you were judged? How did it feel? Take time to reflect and journal about it. Then make a commitment to never do or say anything that might make someone else feel how you felt.

IT IS NOT OUR DIFFERENCES THAT DIVIDE US. IT IS OUR INABILITY TO RECOGNIZE, ACCEPT, AND CELEBRATE THOSE DIFFERENCES.

—Audre Lorde

THIS WEEK...
CELEBRATE CHANGE

TAKE ACTION

FOR YOUR COMMUNITY: In the spirit of acceptance, what is one thing you and your family would like to see improve in your community? Have something in mind? Great. Now commit to helping make that change a reality. Remember, we all have the power to create change.

FOR YOUR FAMILY: Families, like companies, have cultures. These cultures are created over time by thoughts, feelings, and behaviors of the collective. As a family, take inventory of your family culture. Think about it. Discuss it. Collectively agree to change anything that needs a tune-up. Then change and celebrate it.

FOR YOU: What is a change you have always wanted to make but haven't yet? Possibly a New Year's resolution gone wrong? Possibly being a little more of this or a little less of that? Now is your time. Make the change, then celebrate the heck out of it.

> **IF NOTHING EVER CHANGED, THERE'D BE NO BUTTERFLIES.**
>
> —Unknown

Change is inevitable. That doesn't mean we necessarily like it, but it does suggest that we should, because it isn't going anywhere. But why don't we like change? Is it because we are creatures of habit? Is it because it conjures feelings of loss? Or is it because it might challenge us to rethink old beliefs and opinions that up to that point felt pretty ironclad? Regardless of the reason, we think it's time for all of us to **CELEBRATE CHANGE**. There are things in life we can control and things we can't. It is often the ones we can't control that cause us the most pain and anxiety. We have all certainly experienced this recently. But just as there is change that happens to us, there is also change that we can make happen. What changes do you wish to see for yourself, your family, your community, or the world? What changes are we all willing to make in the spirit of creating a better world for everyone? What morals and values are we going to honor and celebrate like never before? This is why change is exciting. It allows us to grow when we accept it and to do and be better when we create it. Celebrating change matters.

What matters most to you? Big question, we know. But we believe it is one of the most important questions we can ask. Because to live a life that is aligned with our priorities and is filled with meaning and purpose, we need to know how to answer this question. If not, bright, shiny objects easily distract us, or we fall victim to simply living and surviving instead of thriving. Well, we want everyone to feel like they are living a life of significance and fulfillment, so we want you to **KNOW WHAT MATTERS MOST**. On average, we spend 8.6 hours a day working or doing work-related tasks, 7.6 hours sleeping, 2.6 hours on leisure activities, 1.1 hours doing household chores, 1.1 hours eating and drinking, 1.2 hours caring for others, and 1.8 hours doing miscellaneous things, including sitting in traffic. At the same time, when asked what matters most, we usually put family at the top of the list. But how much of our jam-packed days do we actually spend quality time with or on our families? Since we can't add more hours to our days, we need to create other solutions in order to embrace and enjoy this thing that matters so much to us. We can do this. We need to do this. Family matters. Knowing what matters most matters.

TAKE ACTION

FOR YOUR COMMUNITY:
How well do you know your neighbors? Unfortunately, polls show only 10 percent of people consider their neighbors friends. Get creative and do something that makes it crystal clear your neighbors and neighborhood know how much they matter to you. Have fun being the connector your community needs.

FOR YOUR FAMILY: Despite constantly feeling busy, we all seem to find time to waste. As a family, if you combined all your wasted minutes throughout the week, you could put them together to create some quality family time. Find the time, get organized, and do something that matters.

FOR YOU: Plan something this week that centers on what matters most to you. Maybe it is going for a thirty-minute walk or sharing coffee with a dear friend. Put it on your calendar, and make it happen.

> **WHAT MATTERS MOST IS THAT WE LEARN FROM LIVING.**
>
> —Doris Lessing

ASK FOR INPUT

TAKE ACTION

FOR YOUR COMMUNITY:
There is nothing better than an old-fashioned feedback or comment box. Create a feedback or comment box for any community of which you are a member. Make sure everyone knows their input matters and is welcome. We can learn and grow so much more when we encourage inclusivity.

FOR YOUR FAMILY: How are decisions made in your family? Does everyone get an equal voice? Are new and different ideas welcomed from all members? Instead of just telling, let's start asking. It is a beautiful way to make someone feel accepted and that they matter.

FOR YOU: On a scale of one to ten, how well do you welcome feedback? Why or why not? Take time to journal, reflect on, or talk about the reasons we either welcome or avoid feedback. Then find a way to welcome it more often.

FEEDBACK IS THE BREAKFAST OF CHAMPIONS.

—Ken Blanchard

We love to judge. We love to react. Now that everyone has a platform via social media, we have the capability to post comments and reactions with virtually zero accountability and a ton of vitriol. It's as if our culture has become addicted to scouring social media with the sole purpose of finding things to reject. It's pretty easy to hide behind an account and say whatever we please. But how often do we welcome what people think of us? How often do we concern ourselves with our own personal approval ratings? This week, **ASK FOR INPUT**. When was the last time you said something to someone and asked how it made him or her feel? When was the last time you approached your teacher, spouse, neighbor, or boss and asked them how you could do a better job? A little unsettling maybe? Well, it's time for all of us to stop letting everyone else know how we feel about what they say and do and to shift the perspective inward. Start with yourself. Part of learning to accept one another is getting a clearer understanding of and learning to accept ourselves. Awareness is powerful. Asking for input matters.

MONDAY GETS CONSISTENT

Things change. But just as things change, there is a ton that stays the same. Fortunately for all of us, the sun rises and sets each and every day. We look forward to Taco Tuesdays each week and pumpkin spice lattes every autumn. This consistency matters, and it shows up in several parts of our lives. Maybe you have a family member who makes your lunch every day or a friend you can always call when you're feeling down. Maybe a sibling consistently shares a corny joke at dinner, or you have a parent who always gives you a massive hug before you leave for school. This is consistency. It is what shapes our skills, habits, and mindsets and creates beautiful masterpieces and symphonies. When it comes to our relationships, it is also the very thing that builds trust. When we show up consistently in our characters, it allows people to know and trust who we truly are. Let's cherish and create consistency in all parts of our lives, both big and small. Being consistent matters.

THIS WEEK...
BE PATIENT

We live in a culture of instant everything. We put a bag of corn kernels in the microwave, and in less than two minutes, we have a giant bowl of hot buttered popcorn. We use our smartphones and devices to order something on the internet, and it's at our doors within twenty-four hours. When trying to walk across a street at an intersection with a traffic light, we press the walk button multiple times, thinking it will speed things up. Not everything is supposed to be quick and easy. This week, we need to **BE PATIENT**. Have you ever planted a vegetable garden? There is something so magical about putting the seeds in the ground, watering and caring for the plants while they grow, then eventually picking and enjoying the fresh vegetables. It takes time and consistency, but the rewards are that much greater. So where in your life might you benefit from practicing a little more patience? Where can you release your tight squeeze on something and simply surrender to and trust in the process? Legacies, relationships, and purpose are lifelong achievements that we foster and appreciate by consistently showing up and patiently helping them grow. This is the stuff that matters most. Being patient matters.

TAKE ACTION

FOR YOUR COMMUNITY:
Think of a situation that happened recently where maybe you got a little impatient with someone in your community. Make it right by acknowledging your behavior with them and letting them know how much they matter to you. It will feel good for you and for them.

FOR YOUR FAMILY: Our patience with one another is often tested because we set ourselves up for failure and frustration. Create a family plan that helps you get on the same page and builds in more clarity, margin, and realistic expectations. Then watch and enjoy as the impatience melts away.

FOR YOU: What is one area in your life where you are not very patient with yourself? What can you do to change this up? How can you begin appreciating the significance of consistency and patience in achieving one of your goals?

THE TWO MOST POWERFUL WARRIORS ARE PATIENCE AND TIME.

—Leo Tolstoy

THIS WEEK...
PUT IN THE WORK

TAKE ACTION

FOR YOUR COMMUNITY:
Start a "Put in the Work" club with the goal to inspire each member to put in the work toward something they have always wanted to achieve. Support and inspire one another. Be one another's biggest cheerleaders. Together is always better.

FOR YOUR FAMILY: How do you show up for your family? Are you reliable? Consistent? Ready to contribute? How would everyone in your family answer these questions? Maybe it is time to ask. The answers will help you bond and minimize the potential for resentment over time.

FOR YOU: It is said it takes ten thousand hours to master something. Not sure if you have an extra ten thousand hours, but what about one thousand? What are you ready to dedicate one thousand hours toward? Commit to an hour a day and see where you are 2.7 years from now.

> I'VE ALWAYS BELIEVED THAT IF YOU PUT IN THE WORK, THE RESULTS WILL COME.
>
> —Michael Jordan

We have all heard the saying "no pain, no gain." But if we were being honest, we would rather it went something like "no pain, no pain" or "no pain, all gain." We hate pain, so we avoid it at all cost. However, we love to gain and wish there was a quick way to achieve it, but there isn't. Anything and everything that matters to us takes time. It takes dedication and consistency. So in the spirit of accomplishing awesome things, this week, we are going to **PUT IN THE WORK**. Ask any professional athlete. Ask any super talented musician. Ask anyone who excels at anything in their life. They will all make sure to share with you how much work it took and that they certainly were not an overnight sensation. We love this, because if you read between the lines, they are almost glad it took so much work. They are proud of the blood, sweat, and tears, because that is how they earned it. So what is something you want to achieve? Are you ready and willing to go the extra mile for it? This doesn't mean you need to be the best in the world at it, but it does mean you have committed to get better. We hope you are excited to get after it. Putting in the work matters.

THIS WEEK...
BELIEVE IN BOUNDARIES

Does it feel like the line between work and life has blurred a little bit? Has the need for personal space, both at home and out in public, been top of mind at all lately? How disciplined have you been when it comes to making healthy choices for yourself physically, mentally, and emotionally? See, uncertain and shifting times can feel like a full-on assault on our boundaries, and if we are not aware of it, we can quickly find ourselves swirling and feeling ungrounded. So this week, let's **BELIEVE IN BOUNDARIES** again. Healthy boundaries are everything. They help us make smart decisions, because we are clear on what is right and wrong, good or bad. They strengthen families, friendships, and relationships, because they allow people to get to know us better and allow us to better understand them. And they allow us to stick to plans and achieve what we set out to accomplish, because they keep us focused and structured. A world without boundaries is complete chaos. Just imagine driving without lanes or speed limits. Well, a life or a family without them is pretty messy too. Treat your boundaries like they are precious, and respect those of people around you. Believing in boundaries matters.

TAKE ACTION

FOR YOUR COMMUNITY:
How actively engaged is your neighborhood in watching out for one another? This could mean noticing something that looks suspicious or simply that someone's sprinkler is broken. Your neighborhood is your community. Protect it and work together to keep things in order.

FOR YOUR FAMILY: Every family needs healthy boundaries that are understood and respected. Has your family established clear boundaries? Do they work for everyone? Can they be improved? Maybe it is time for a solid family conversation about creating or refreshing your individual and family boundaries.

FOR YOU: Have you developed any bad habits in the past year or so? On the flip side, have you picked up any new, good ones? It's time to put up two new boundaries—one to protect you from the bad habit and one to nurture the new one.

WALLS KEEP EVERYBODY OUT. BOUNDARIES TEACH PEOPLE WHERE THE DOOR IS.

—Mark Groves

27

THIS WEEK...
HONOR YOUR WORD

TAKE ACTION

FOR YOUR COMMUNITY: We have lost faith in our institutions because we no longer believe in or trust what they say. Create a letter-writing campaign, and get people to send a letter to your local leadership to make it crystal clear that all of you expect them to honor their word.

FOR YOUR FAMILY: Play "Paying for Good." The rules are simple: If you are late to or don't show up at a family function, it will cost you. If you don't honor your word...yep, another charge. At the end of the month, donate the money to a local cause your family is passionate about.

FOR YOU: Do a tune-up on your personal reminder system. Do you even have a system in place? A calendar? An app? No matter what your system is, make sure it works for you, and set yourself up to be a follow-through machine.

> **YOUR WORD IS YOUR HONOR. IF YOU SAY YOU'RE GOING TO DO SOMETHING, THEN YOU NEED TO DO IT.**
>
> —Joyce Meyer

All of us have made plans to have lunch with a friend, to meet with a customer or colleague, or to begrudgingly go to the dentist. We have also all said we would call someone back in those infamous "five minutes." On the surface, pretty straightforward stuff here. Yet as the day for your lunch or meeting grew near, did you ever start to feel a little doubt? Like there might be a late cancellation or a no-show? Did you feel the need to reach out "just to confirm" your plans? Why is that? Because our culture has now entered what is called the "post-truth" era. In other words, our words are quickly becoming something far less trustworthy than they once were. This week and every week going forward, we think it's time to **HONOR YOUR WORD**. Our words are everything. If we can't be trusted to keep our commitments and follow through, then creating meaningful relationships and healthy families is simply impossible. So let's strive to be that person who no one ever has to question. No need for reminders or confirmations. Let your dentist know they don't need to text you every day to remind you about your upcoming appointment. Let your family know that you do as you say, and watch your respect-o-meter go way up. Honoring your word matters.

MONDAY GETS HEALTHY

Our physical and mental health must be our first priority, but are they? It's pretty simple stuff here, because without our health, we have nothing. Harsh but true. But why is it that we take our health for granted so easily? Most of the time, we don't need to think about how our hearts pump blood, how our lungs expand and contract, how our eyes take in what we see, and how our brains process eleven million bits of information every second. But when any of these functions falter or fail, we think about them incessantly. A healthy person has a thousand wishes; an unhealthy person has one—to be healthy. It's time to be proactive about our health. We know better. Living in the information age allows us to have all the information we need in an instant. In other words, the ignorance excuse is forever gone. The question is whether we are genuinely ready to take ownership of our health. Yes, it is an investment. Yes, it takes thought and time and effort. But the rewards and return on investment are immeasurable. Your physical and mental health matter to you, your friends, your family, and the world. Being healthy matters.

THIS WEEK...
TAKE OWNERSHIP

Our personal health starts with us. Our desire and commitment to be healthy is dependent on one person...the one each of us sees in the mirror. Of course there are factors that impact our health, like genetics, disease, economics, and the environment, but we can't blame everything on them. We play a leading role in staying healthy, and that is a role we should all embrace. So this week, we want you to **TAKE OWNERSHIP** of your health. We know what is good for us, but do we do it? We know what is good for our family members, but do we encourage it? Maybe this question will help you take charge: How do you want to look and feel ten years from now? How about twenty or even thirty years from now? Can you see and feel it? We hope so and that it is a picture of pure health—physically, mentally, emotionally, and spiritually. We also hope it is an awesome enough vision that it kick-starts the work today, because you are the author of that story. Make your health a priority, and it will honor you. You may also inspire the rest of your family to do the same. That's the power of leading the way and owning your life. Taking ownership matters.

I DON'T COUNT MY SIT-UPS. I ONLY START COUNTING ONCE IT STARTS HURTING.

—Muhammad Ali

TAKE ACTION

FOR YOUR COMMUNITY: Start a healthy team with members from your community. Maybe it is a walking group or a book club. Maybe it is group yoga, either in person or using video conferencing. As a team, you can improve all aspects of your health. Sounds fun, doesn't it!

FOR YOUR FAMILY: Being healthy as a family is all about being on the same page. No cookies in the cupboard if someone is trying to lose weight. Create a family plan by having everyone express their individual goals and support needs. A healthy family is a loving and supportive family.

FOR YOU: Health wise, what is one thing you have unhappily accepted or blamed on something else? Maybe it is the "I just don't have enough time" thing. Or maybe it is the "Everyone in my family is…" argument. Well, it's time to stop blaming and start owning. No excuses.

THIS WEEK...
PRACTICE PEACE

TAKE ACTION

FOR YOUR COMMUNITY: Say "hello" first, ask the grocery clerk how their day is going, and let the car go in front of you while you wave to the other driver with a big smile on your face. Be the Zen master who spreads peace and calm in your community.

FOR YOUR FAMILY: Does your family operate electronics, or do electronics operate you? It's time for a break from your screens. Start with just one evening a week. No phone, no television, no video games, no screens. Instead, have meaningful conversations, read books, journal, or do a puzzle. Enjoy the QT.

FOR YOU: Take time to journal every day. Pick a new question each time: What brings me joy? Why is it challenging for me to do nothing? What is my hope for the world? If I had one wish, I would wish for... Doesn't it feel meaningful and healthy already? Enjoy.

> **LET GO OF THE PEOPLE WHO DULL YOUR SHINE, POISON YOUR SPIRIT, AND BRING YOU DRAMA.**
>
> —Anonymous

Our mental and emotional health is just as important as our physical health. With a higher prevalence of reported stress, depression, anxiety, and even violence, our mental health is in a fragile state. With the increased use of technology to make our lives easier and more productive, we now pack too much into our days. From the time we wake up to the time our heads hit the pillow, we are plugged in and amped up. It's time for all of us to **PRACTICE PEACE**. Let's first remember that we are human *beings*, not human *doings*. But let's be honest about accepting the fact that we *do* more than we *be*. What would it feel like to not have access to your phone, email, or social media for a week? Think you could do it? How about for even one day? Your answer most likely supports the argument that maybe you need to get off the grid. Maybe your entire family does as well. So take time this week to help yourself and your family slow your roll. Meditate, enjoy nature, breathe, or read a book together. We all need time to rest, recharge, and reset. Practicing peace matters.

CHECK YOUR CHOICES

Merriam-Webster defines choice as "the act of making a selection." Having the ability to make choices is a beautiful thing and should never be taken for granted. Every country or culture has different boundaries on the type and number of choices people can make, and whenever someone's choices are limited by outside forces, we feel a collective loss of freedom in humanity. But just because choices are so abundant in most Western civilizations doesn't mean we necessarily make the best ones. This week, we want you to **CHECK YOUR CHOICES**. The first choice you need to make is whether your health is important to you and your family, because without choosing health, it's really hard to be healthy. The next choice is how to achieve that level of health. This, however, is where things can get confusing for us. Should we eat vegan, vegetarian, paleo, keto, or fruitarian? Should we exercise every day for thirty minutes or three times a week for one hour? Should we sleep seven, eight, nine, or ten hours each night? Don't let this stymie you. Pick a plan and go for it. Then choose to alter or perfect it as you go, because you have that choice as well. Checking your choices matters.

TAKE ACTION

FOR YOUR COMMUNITY: Sadly, too many people don't have access to healthy food or food at all. In other words, their choices are limited. Get involved in a local cause that helps bring healthy options to people in need. Choose to help people have access and healthy options. That is a powerful choice.

FOR YOUR FAMILY: As a family, pick your favorites. What is everyone's favorite fruit? Vegetable? Form of exercise? Hobby? Soul-filling activity? Knowing this information will make it easier to create a healthy lifestyle for your family. Again, it is all about access and options that people enjoy.

FOR YOU: "Oh, I had no idea!" used to work, but thanks to our age of information, not any more. Knowing this, what do you still choose even though you know it's not healthy? Make the choice to choose differently from this moment on. You can do it. Just take ownership.

TAKE CARE OF YOUR BODY. IT'S THE ONLY PLACE YOU HAVE TO LIVE.

—Jim Rohn

37

TAKE ACTION

FOR YOUR COMMUNITY: Know someone who just lost their job or a loved one? Hear about a neighbor who is sick and can't go to the grocery store? Bake them cookies, make them fresh soup, or drop off flowers. Feeling seen and supported by others is one of the quickest remedies for healing a wound.

FOR YOUR FAMILY: Feelings that are pushed down are dangerous. Find ways to allow one another to express emotions, share secrets, and feel feelings. Do a weekly check-in with everyone. Simply ask, "How are you?" Even this is enough to promote sharing and lovingly being there for one another.

FOR YOU: We all have wounds. Some of us are quicker to heal, while some of us try to ignore or strong-arm our sadness. What about you? Is there something you would love to healthily heal? If so, consider talking about it with a trusted family member, friend, or professional. We all could use an "expensive friend" every now and then.

> **WHAT MENTAL HEALTH NEEDS IS MORE SUNLIGHT, MORE CANDOR, MORE UNASHAMED CONVERSATION.**
>
> —Glenn Close

When we have cuts, we clean them. When we have bruises, we ice them. When we strain muscles, we rest. But what happens when our wounds are not physical? What do we do when we have emotional wounds? What do we do if we have experienced suffering or trauma? There are several ways to answer this sensitive question, but one thing we know for sure is that doing nothing is not the healthy choice. So this week, in a super loving and supportive way, we want you to **FEEL THE FEELS**. If you are human, you will experience loss, grief, trauma, judgment, bullying, and pain at some point on your journey. They are just part of life. Over half of us will suffer from a mental illness at some point. This is not something to be taken lightly, because these are real experiences and real emotions. But these wounds should not be kept secret; rather, they need to be treated, just like a broken arm. If you or anyone in your family relate to this, please take the bold step to get the proper help. Find professional support or an empathetic friend or family member. Take a break from the pain, find a creative outlet, get out in nature, or volunteer somewhere. Most importantly, know that there is hope and things can and will get better. Feeling your feelings fully matters.

MONDAY GETS LOVING

How would you answer this question: "In one word, what do you think we need more of in our world today?" If you are like the thousands of people we have asked to answer this question, there is a good chance the word "love" came to mind. This makes us wonder though. Are people saying we need more love because there can never be too much of it, or because they sadly feel like we have lost our loving ways? Well, either way, the message is clear, so let's dedicate an entire month to being more loving. Love is the most powerful force in the world. Nothing can make us feel happier and more hopeful yet bring us to our knees so harshly at the same time. That's why the idea of a family carries so much weight. That's the risk, but it's worth it. Because a life without love is also a life without empathy, compassion, gratitude, thankfulness, kindness, and care. Which means it is also a life without healthy families. So let's all chip in this month to let love shine on ourselves, our families, and our communities. Being loving matters.

THIS WEEK...
ASK QUESTIONS

There is a super basic form of expressing love that has fallen somewhat dormant. We don't think this is because we have become less loving; at least we hope not. But we do believe we have gotten a little too wrapped up in our own lives, which stands in great opposition to this particular expression of love. Because this expression requires us to completely get out of our own heads and to genuinely invest in someone else. This week, we want you to **ASK QUESTIONS**. If there is one thing we have all learned recently, it's that the question "How are you?" is no longer a throwaway question that can be shrugged off. Nope. Words like "good," "fine," and "okay" are just not enough. But when is the last time someone asked you more than just "How are you?" When have you asked someone more than that? How about questions like "What was the highlight of your week?" "What are you most excited about for the future?" "What is your greatest fear?" "If you had one wish, what would it be?" Asking these questions and actively listening to the answers is a true expression of love. It lets someone know you care deeply about who they are more than what they do. So get your questions and ears ready. Asking questions matters.

> **I JUST LOVE ASKING QUESTIONS. I LOVE PEOPLE. IT'S IN MY DNA. I'M CURSED— AND BLESSED.**
>
> —Larry King

TAKE ACTION

FOR YOUR COMMUNITY: As a family, spend the week asking other people in your community, "In one word, what is one thing you think we need more of in our community?" At the end of the month, create a word cloud, and share it with those you asked. Then generate more of all of it together.

FOR YOUR FAMILY: Ask every family member to share one question they would like to be asked the most often. This is hopefully the question that makes them feel the most loved by the rest of you. Once everyone has their personal question, make a promise to ask one another their question more often.

FOR YOU: Are you good at asking other people questions? Write down five to ten questions you would feel comfortable asking anyone. Then remember these questions and ask them whenever the opportunity arises. Of course, feel free to grow the list or go off script as well.

THIS WEEK...
MAKE TIME

TAKE ACTION

FOR YOUR COMMUNITY: There are people in your community starving for love, and nothing communicates love more than the giving of your time. Do some research, and find a volunteer opportunity for your family. Be of service, and deliver love to those who might need it most.

FOR YOUR FAMILY: If your family was awarded one extra hour this week to do something meaningful and loving together, what would you do? Discuss it, and settle on your answer. Next step: go do it this month, and enjoy every second of it. Sometimes we have to make time.

FOR YOU: What is one thing you absolutely love to do? This is that thing that warms your soul and is almost like giving yourself the best gift ever. Promise you will find the time to enjoy that "me" time this week. You are worth the time. You matter.

IT'S NOT ABOUT HAVING TIME. IT'S ABOUT MAKING TIME.

— Anonymous

When people are asked how they would have lived any stage of their life differently or what they regret the most, their answers usually relate to how they spent their time. Some of the most common responses include "I wish I hadn't worked so hard," "I wish I had stayed in better touch with my friends," "I wish I had spent more time with the ones I love the most," or "I wish I had pursued my passions more." So in the spirit of love, it's time for all of us to **MAKE TIME**. It isn't necessarily easy to accept, but time is not infinite when it comes to our journeys on this planet. We each get 1,440 minutes a day and hopefully get to enjoy as many days as possible. But living without regrets starts with our choices right here and now. Spending time on ourselves to pursue our passions, live more authentically, and find more joy and happiness matters. Spending time with and being more present with our children and elders matters. So take this opportunity to be mindful of each and every moment and make sure you are making enough time for the things that matter most to you. Really love every time you walk your dog or pet your cat. Really love every meal you have with your family. Really love laughing and playing and having fun. And do more of all of it. Making time matters.

We are curators of our lives. None of us starts in the same place or get to the same place, but we all have the ability to choose, some more than others, and there is a certain level of agency in each of us. Much like a curator in a museum who selects the art, organizes the exhibit, and holds great responsibility and accountability for all of it, we get to do the same. Why? Because we matter. Our actions, words, and thoughts all matter. And from this place of self-empowerment, guided by the need for more love in our lives, we can also **CURATE COMPASSION**. There are people all over the world who need our love, concern, and support. This might be someone in our families or a friend. It might be a total stranger. Or it might be a group of people halfway around the world. But let's not let our paradigm for compassion be based on pity or sympathy. This isn't a matter of less than or more than. This is purely a manner of understanding that we are all humans. We all play for the same team. And when one of us hurts, we all do. Compassion understands that when we raise the water level, all boats rise. It's a "we" thing. It's a family thing. So let's look outside ourselves to bring more compassion to everyone and everything. Curating compassion matters.

TAKE ACTION

FOR YOUR COMMUNITY: What is a challenge in your community that has always saddened you or put a pit in your stomach? Maybe it is homelessness or something for the animals? Make a commitment to do one thing to make a positive impact on the cause you've chosen.

FOR YOUR FAMILY: All families are different and have different ways of relating. Some go for the tough-love approach, while others embrace the you-can-do-no-wrong approach. Regardless of your approach, consider how much compassion you curate within your family. Then discuss ways to create a little more of it.

FOR YOU: Take a moment to write down five things you do well. Once you have your five things, take a second moment to compliment yourself out loud for each of them. Try standing in front of the mirror and saying your first name before each compliment to really feel it.

> **BE KIND, FOR EVERYONE YOU MEET IS FIGHTING A HARD BATTLE.**
>
> —Ian MacLaren

THIS WEEK...
CHOOSE KINDNESS

TAKE ACTION

FOR YOUR COMMUNITY: As a family, paint kindness rocks and place them around your neighborhood. Just make sure you place them in high-traffic, yet safe places where people will surely enjoy them. Watch how quickly they become the talk of your block.

FOR YOUR FAMILY: Create a kindness poster together. It can include images of kind acts, words or sayings that spread kindness, or drawings of things that are kind. Take your time with it, and consider framing and hanging it when you are finished.

FOR YOU: Do one additional kind thing for yourself this week. You pick.

> **KINDNESS IS A LANGUAGE THE DUMB CAN SPEAK AND THE DEAF CAN HEAR AND UNDERSTAND.**
>
> —Christian Nestell Bovee

Let's set the record straight: there is nothing random about kindness. Kindness is intentional, and it is inspired by a thought, then a choice, and then an act. In the split second when someone decides to open a door for someone else, they are choosing kindness. The moment someone picks up their phone to call a friend going through a rough time, they are choosing kindness. The time that a group of students or employees volunteers at a local agency to give back to their community, they are choosing kindness. So let's reframe how we talk about kindness. Instead of calling it random, let's **CHOOSE KINDNESS**. Doesn't that feel better? Doesn't that make you want to make it more prevalent in your life? Because kindness changes everything. It creates fulfillment and purpose. It creates connection and community, and it can even be the catalyst to create more kindness. Yes, ripple effects are real, and kind ones are the best. So let's rally the family to be kindness gurus. Let's all wake up every morning with the intention of spreading as much kindness as we can. Just think about how amazing that will be. Choosing kindness matters.

MONDAY GETS MINDFUL

The terms *mindfulness* and *being mindful* have become more prevalent in our world. Maybe it's in response to our increasingly fast-paced lifestyle. Maybe it's COVID-19. Maybe it's the massive social and political divide we have all experienced. There are countless books about being mindful. There are websites, coaches, therapies, and apps. And life is truly amazing when we are able to be mindful and present in every moment. But this isn't necessarily easy, and there is a good reason why. Our conscious brains process forty to fifty bits of information per second. Our unconscious brains process slightly more than eleven million bits of information per second. Our eyes process ten million bits, our skin one million, our ears and nose one hundred thousand, and our taste one thousand. Not only does this inform us of why it is so challenging to be present, it also illustrates our need to create moments of peace and quiet. Being mindful matters.

THIS WEEK...
ENJOY THE NOW

Life can be filled with wonder one moment and downright despair the next. It can literally change in the blink of an eye. And just as you read this sentence in the present, it just became your past, as you are on to the next sentence. Again, it happen that quickly. So with the number of moments in our pasts building rapidly and the number of moments yet to come in our futures shrinking rapidly, the best thing we can do is focus on the precious present moment that is in front of us right now. So this week, we want you to **ENJOY THE NOW**. Life is not about the woulda, shoulda, couldas. Living in the past will get us nowhere. No more saying, "It felt like yesterday when…" It's also not about wondering or being anxious about the future. We can't slow down the ticks on a clock, but we can slow down the moments between each tick. We can be more present. We can literally train our brains to shut out the noise and the distractions, to focus all our senses on the here and now, and to fill our hearts with gratitude for the gift of life. Even when life gets hard, we can trust there is a reason for it and that one day, what hurts today will make us better tomorrow. So enjoy all of it. Enjoying the now matters.

TAKE ACTION

FOR YOUR COMMUNITY: Your community has so much to offer, whether it is a park, a walking trail, restaurants, museums, farmers markets, or cafés. Go enjoy them. Help your community thrive by actively participating in it today. Like right now.

FOR YOUR FAMILY: What drives you nuts about your family? Make a list of the top ten—dishes in the sink, carpooling, too much noise. Now, find a way to shift your paradigm and dig deep to find joy, appreciation, and laughter in those experiences. One day, you will miss all of them.

FOR YOU: Take a moment every single day to get quiet and breathe in gratitude. Even in the toughest of times, we can find it. Let us never forget everything we have to be grateful for in our lives.

"WHAT DAY IS IT?" ASKED POOH. "IT'S TODAY," SQUEAKED PIGLET. "MY FAVORITE DAY," SAID POOH.

—A. A. Milne

BE INTENTIONAL

TAKE ACTION

FOR YOUR COMMUNITY: How can your family be better neighbors? There is your intention. You get to decide how to make it happen. Mr. Rogers is smiling already.

FOR YOUR FAMILY: Create an "Intention for the Week" system for your family. Each week, let a family member pick the intention for the week, like "to laugh more," "to communicate better," or "to plant a new tree." Everyone join forces to bring each intention to life.

FOR YOU: When is the last time you made an intention? Been a minute? Great. It's time for a new one. What do you intend to accomplish? Who do you intend to be? How do you intend to grow? Now place your intention and stay true to it. Enjoy living intentionally.

OUR INTENTION CREATES OUR REALITY.

—Wayne Dyer

Have you ever thought about why you do what you do? Why do you eat? Why do you shower? Why do you mow the lawn or call a friend? It is super easy to go on autopilot and just do things without connecting to the true reason. Well, we want to remind you that everything you do is for a purpose. Some of them are simple ones, like the fact that we brush our teeth because we don't want cavities. But some of them are a bit more profound, and that is what this week is all about. It's time to **BE INTENTIONAL**. Intention is defined as "a determination to act in a certain way." To take it a step further, determination is defined as "a firmness of purpose; resoluteness." So intentions are not something to be taken lightly. They are not just a wish or a "wouldn't it be nice if" sort of thing. They are meaningful and require action, resolve, and determination. So what is one intention you have for yourself, either personally or professionally? What is one intention you have for your family? What is one intention you have for the world? Whatever it is or they are, let's all set the intention to be more intentional in our lives. Being intentional matters.

UNPLUG TO PLUG IN

There was a time when the majority of electrical sockets in our homes were mostly left unused, other than the occasional lamp here or there and a toaster or alarm clock. Those days are a distant memory. Now we have power strips in most of our sockets in order to have more access to electrical power. We need more sockets for more gadgets—cell phone chargers, internet modems, Wi-Fi extenders, computers, home security systems, air purifiers, smart home devices, and the newly famous Instant Pot, now with a Wi-Fi option. So literally, we are plugged in more than ever before. Additionally, we have emailing, FaceTiming, texting, instant messaging, and social media posting that seemingly allow us to be more plugged in to one another's lives. Then why do we feel more disconnected than ever before? Well, it's because we are. This week, it's time to **UNPLUG TO PLUG IN**. Isolation and disconnection from one another are hurting us badly. We are losing touch with what it means to be in relationship with one another, in other words, what it means to be human. We need one another. Our families need us. Our communities need us. Let's reconnect by disconnecting. We are designed for this. Unplugging to plug in matters.

> **ALMOST EVERYTHING WILL WORK AGAIN IF YOU UNPLUG IT FOR A FEW MINUTES, INCLUDING YOU.**
>
> —Anne Lamott

TAKE ACTION

FOR YOUR COMMUNITY: As a family, add together all the minutes your phones show that you were on social media for the past week. Once you have that number, commit to volunteering in your community for that many minutes next week instead of doing social media. Oh, and don't bring your phones.

FOR YOUR FAMILY: During family dinners, create a stack of everyone's phones on the table, facing down. If any member picks up their phone, they have to do the dishes for a week. Keep it going until someone just can't resist. Soon, you will form a new habit of no phones during dinner.

FOR YOU: Take a break from social media for the week. Don't look at it, don't post on it, and turn off your notices. You can even announce it if that makes you feel better. Just try it and see how it feels. Wonder what you will discover.

SIMPLIFY YOUR LIFE

TAKE ACTION

FOR YOUR COMMUNITY: There is a good chance your family has something you don't need or use—business suits, socks, shoes, extra computers or cell phones. Bless someone else and bless yourself through the act of giving and also simplifying your life. This is a win-win.

FOR YOUR FAMILY: On a scale of one to ten, with ten being high, how complex (hectic) is your family's schedule? We figured so. Gather the troops; it's time to streamline the chaos. Let simplicity lead the way.

FOR YOU: What can you start saying no to? We often want to please everyone, so it is challenging to say no to someone. But at the end of the day, you are letting yourself and your life down by always saying yes. Just give it a shot and see what happens.

THE HEIGHT OF SOPHISTICATION IS SIMPLICITY.

—Clare Boothe Luce

Work. Exercise. Bills. Social media. Traffic. Weddings. Pets. Health. Friendships. Food. Kids. Housework. Emails. Practice. Homework. Hobbies. Illness. Birthday parties. In any given day, week, or month, most of us have a ton of responsibilities and are constantly bombarded by them. It's no wonder that "If I only had more time" or "If I just had two of me" are such common phrases. So it shouldn't come as a surprise that we often feel out of balance. Well, this week, we are going to do something about it. It's time to **SIMPLIFY YOUR LIFE**. Simplifying is one of the key steps toward achieving mindfulness, and a big part of simplifying is prioritizing what is important to you, what is necessary, and how you want to spend your time. Simplifying doesn't always mean you need to throw everything out. Instead, it means spending time identifying what is helpful and what brings you joy and saying goodbye to the rest. And in the process, it's important to remember that letting go of things, whether those are belongings, habits, or other responsibilities, is a natural and incredibly healthy part of life. Create more space for good in your life by letting the rest go. You can do it. Simplifying your life matters.

MONDAY GETS CONNECTED

We live in an interesting time. Search Google for words like *connect*, *connected*, or *connection*, and most of your findings will help you better understand the internet, Wi-Fi, and how to improve your internet speed. Of course being connected to the grid is a big part of our lives today, but this is not the kind of connection to focus on this month. Rather, we want to talk about human connection—the relationships between two or more people that take place off-line. This form of connection is not just nice, it's necessary. Though it's not always easy, we are designed to live in community and in relationship with one another. And while technology has made it easier to connect with others, this doesn't mean we are building meaningful connections or relationships. So get ready to find new ways to get connected as a family and a community. It is one thing to live together in a house. It is something far more meaningful to turn that house into a home. We do this by seeing one another, creating new experiences together, and truly loving and accepting one another. Being connected matters.

MAKE A MEMORY

Do you remember when you first learned to swim? Do you remember your first pet? Do you remember your first...? See, we can go on forever here: day of high school, job, time driving, best friend, bicycle. There is something about the word *first* that instantly creates a special moment that we never forget. These moments become our lives' stories, our families' stories. These moments are what scrapbooks are built from and that create the "Year in Review" Facebook video that we all love to share. So this week, it's pretty simple: we want you to **MAKE A MEMORY**. So many options and choices to make. Where will you go? What will you do? Who will join you? When will you go? But isn't this the fun of it? How creative can you and your family get this week? We are dying to know. So how about this? Whatever you do, we would love for you to post a few photos using the hashtag #EveryMondayMatters. However, we say this with a small caveat: please don't spend too much time taking photos. The focus should be on the experience itself and the memories you create together. Enjoy. Making a memory matters.

TAKE ACTION

FOR YOUR COMMUNITY:
A family that serves together stays together. Make a monthly commitment to volunteer in your community. It will make a memory for not only you and your family but also those you serve. It just might inspire other families to join you and make their own new memories.

FOR YOUR FAMILY: As a family, think about something meaningful you can do together. Ideally, it will be a first for everyone, just to make it that much more fun. Cherish every moment along the way.

FOR YOU: Write a story about one of the greatest memories of your life. Write it is as though someone will read it and get to connect with just how special a moment it was. Then share it with your family.

> ## EACH DAY OF OUR LIVES WE MAKE DEPOSITS IN THE MEMORY BANKS OF OUR CHILDREN.
>
> —Charles R. Swindoll

63

THIS WEEK...
OPEN THE DOOR

TAKE ACTION

FOR YOUR COMMUNITY: Have you ever attended a town hall meeting in your community? Did you know you are always welcome? Grab the family and go attend one. Share your thoughts during the meeting, and listen to what other community members have to say. It's a great way to connect with your community.

FOR YOUR FAMILY: Establish an open-door policy with your family. If it helps, put some structure and guidelines to it in the beginning to help ease into it. Open-door policies come with a lot of trust, respect, and honor. They need to be constructive and appreciated, not abused.

FOR YOU: Are you holding on to something that weighs heavy on your heart? This is not healthy for you. Find a friend or family member or a trusted third party, and get it out. It's time to let it go so you can grow. Open your heart and set it free.

COMMUNICATION LEADS TO COMMUNITY—THAT IS, TO UNDERSTANDING, INTIMACY, AND THE MUTUAL VALUING THAT WAS PREVIOUSLY LACKING.

—Rollo May

There is a concept we often hear used in organizations called the open-door policy. This policy is often communicated by people in leadership positions as a way of letting their employees know they are accessible and open for conversation. If it works so well in organizations, don't you think it might also work well in families? We do. This week, we want you to **OPEN THE DOOR**. Being able to express ourselves and share our thoughts and feelings is vital for all of us. We all want to feel like we have a voice and that our voice is actually heard by others, especially those people who mean the most to us, like our families. Does your family welcome input from everyone? Does your family create a space where everyone can share what is on their mind and in their heart? If not, this is the perfect week for you. The health of your family is only as good as the health of each individual in it. We know that secrets are our sickness and that not feeling valued only leads to mental health issues, resentment, and disconnection. So as a family, we need to do all we can to avoid this. Let's welcome and celebrate open communication. Let's connect deeper. Opening the door matters.

VALUE TRADITION

Do you ever wonder why your father works so hard? Why your mom won't leave the house without putting on lipstick first? Or why your grandfather always stands in the doorway and waves until he can no longer see your car as you drive away? There is a good chance that all these behaviors were learned. This is also the reason your family serves your great-grandma's famous stuffing that no one seems to have a written recipe for every Thanksgiving. Yes, this week, take time to **VALUE TRADITION** and embrace your family's story. How well do you know your family's history? The history of your own culture? The family traditions that may or may not have been passed down through the generations? There is real power in knowing where you come from, even if the story isn't perfect. When we know the joys and struggles of our ancestors, we start to learn a little bit more about ourselves— our habits, our dreams, and our hopes for the world. Each one of us is made up of all the people who came before us, and taking the time to get to know where we came from and who they were helps us take ownership over our own lives and identities. Valuing tradition matters.

CHANGE YOUR OPINIONS, KEEP TO YOUR PRINCIPLES; CHANGE YOUR LEAVES, KEEP INTACT YOUR ROOTS.

—Victor Hugo

TAKE ACTION

FOR YOUR COMMUNITY: Do you know the history of the city or state in which you live? Well, it's time to. As a family, make it a fun and interactive learning experience. My guess is that it will bring a lot more meaning and pride to the place you call home.

FOR YOUR FAMILY: Think of five questions to ask each of your family members. For example: "What is your favorite childhood memory?" "What are you most proud of about yourself?" "How did Grandma and Grandpa meet?" Write down your answers and keep asking questions; it's all part of your family's story.

FOR YOU: What is one thing you have always wanted to learn about your family's history? Great. Now get to the bottom of it. Don't regret never asking about days gone by.

GO WITH GRACE

TAKE ACTION

FOR YOUR COMMUNITY: Communities are made up of people. People have different beliefs, values, opinions, and backgrounds. More people, more variety. The key is being able to listen, learn, and understand one another. This cannot happen without grace. So have graceful conversations. Connect gracefully with those who seem different from you.

FOR YOUR FAMILY: We all make mistakes, but how we respond to these occurrences plays a major role in how well we connect as a family. If we all want to be forgiven, then we also need to forgive. Make grace one of the pillars of your family.

FOR YOU: We are often harder on ourselves than we are on other people. What are some unloving thoughts you have about yourself? How is your self-talk? Make incremental changes to be kinder to yourself. People love you and believe in you, maybe even more than you do yourself.

> WORDS CAN SOMETIMES, IN MOMENTS OF GRACE, ATTAIN THE QUALITY OF DEEDS.
>
> —Elie Wiesel

There are many definitions for grace, but what we're playing with this week is a feeling of tenderness, a feeling of vulnerability, and the act of stepping lightly with lots of space for forgiving others (and ourselves). This is the kind of grace that knows there is a difference between being right and being kind and that sometimes, if not most times, it's better to be kind than right. So get ready to feel something extremely freeing, because this week, we want you to **GO WITH GRACE**. The beautiful thing about grace is that we can build more of it into our lives, and it starts with gratefulness. When we focus on gratitude and what we're grateful for, grace starts to seep in. We can start being kinder and more generous to others and ourselves. We can allow others to make mistakes, and we can have compassion and understanding toward them. We also get to remember that we want others to do the same for us when we mess up. Grace opens up a sweet space for emotions and feelings and lets them move through us without judgment or fear. When we live lives of gratitude, grace walks hand in hand with us, allowing the world and others to be as they are and letting us find ways to contribute as we can. Going with grace matters.

MONDAY GETS SPECTACULAR

Spectacular. Isn't that a great word? What do you find spectacular? When is the last time you even thought or used the word *spectacular*? Well, regardless of your answer, we say, "spectacular," and you are going to be saying it quite a bit this month too. Each of us plays two roles when it comes to the idea of being spectacular. In one sense, there is already so much around us that is worthy of our attention, our awe, and our wonder. We just need to do a better job of seeing and celebrating it. On the flip side, there is also too much in our culture that is negative, uninspiring, and ugly, so we need to counter this with everything that is awesome, uplifting, and good. So get ready to create a bunch of spectacular this month. We are going to focus on creating awesomeness. We are going to feel the energy all around us and better understand what we contribute to it. We are going to own our power, plan for the best, and move forward full steam ahead. There is no better time than right now to go for it. Being spectacular matters.

THIS WEEK...
FEEL THE WONDER

In 1963, Andy Williams recorded a new song and gave a new reputation to the holidays as "The Most Wonderful Time of the Year." You might be singing his song in your head right now after simply reading the title of it. Yes, we agree the holidays are wonderful, but we also love the idea that any time of the year can be the most wonderful. Wonder doesn't know time and space...or the calendar, for that matter. Wonder is energy. A feeling. A force that lifts our spirits and invites us to see and feel things bigger than life. Wonder is magic. So this week, we want you to **FEEL THE WONDER**. Take a moment to reflect on the power of wonder. Everything we see in our world, whether in a physical state or an achievement, started from a place of wonder. "I wonder what it would be like to walk on the moon." "I wonder what it would take to build a fully electric car." So what do you wonder about? For you? For your family? Or what wonders around you grab your attention and move your soul? Butterflies? The fall leaves? This week is about being open to seeing and creating more wonder. With a click of the heels and the wave of our wands, let's enjoy the magic. Feeling the wonder matters.

TAKE ACTION

FOR YOUR COMMUNITY: Even if you live in the heart of a major city, somewhere around, you can find nature. Grab your family, and go enjoy the wonder of nature. It is one of the most spectacular and right-sizing things you can do. Be in awe and wonder.

FOR YOUR FAMILY: Make a family greatest hits list of moments and experiences you have shared together. Relive those moments. Laugh about them. Reconnect with the wonder you all felt. Reflecting on the wonder helps keep it alive.

FOR YOU: In the spirit of being spectacular, finish the statement, "I wonder if I could…" Perfect. Know that you can, and make it happen. Feel it, believe it, make it real.

THE UNIVERSE IS FULL OF MAGICAL THINGS PATIENTLY WAITING FOR OUR WITS TO GROW SHARPER.

—Eden Phillpotts

THIS WEEK...
OWN YOUR AWESOMENESS

TAKE ACTION

FOR YOUR COMMUNITY: If someone asked you what your favorite thing is about your community, what would you say? Maybe it's the restaurants? Maybe it's the people? Maybe it's the architecture? Once you have your answer, grab your family, and go enjoy more of that favorite thing. Your community is waiting.

FOR YOUR FAMILY: Every family needs a family cheer or song. Gather together and write yours. Who knows? You might be starting a new family tradition. It's going to be awesome.

FOR YOU: The ways you sit, stand, and hold your head and your arms all have direct impacts on how you feel about yourself. The opposite is true as well. So stand tall. Chin high. Arms open. Eyes peeled. Now, throw on a cape. This is what awesome looks like.

> **WHEN YOU'RE TRUE TO WHO YOU ARE, AMAZING THINGS HAPPEN.**
>
> —Deborah Norville

You are amazing. You probably don't hear that enough, but you are. And even if you do hear that from people, there's a good chance you don't necessarily feel or own it. After all, sometimes compliments are a little tough for us to receive and embrace. Well, it's time for that to change. You are awesome. You are one of a kind. Your presence in life makes the world unique. Of the nearly eight billion people in the world, there is only one *you*. Not one of us is similar in all the same ways, and that's a beautiful thing. So this week, we want you to discover what makes you you and finally **OWN YOUR AWESOMENESS**. Let's be clear that being awesome doesn't mean a quest for perfection. We are awesome in our flaws, just as we are in the places we excel. They are all part of these perfectly imperfect packages that make us who we are. We just need to discover and embrace how spectacular we are so we can bring our whole selves to our relationships, families, work, school, and lives. Never forget that at the end of the day, your greatest superpower is just being you. This week, discover that confidence comes from within, own it, and share it with the rest of us. Owning your awesomeness matters.

THIS WEEK...
PREPARE TO LAUNCH

For the lucky few, being or achieving spectacular just sort of happens. We've all heard the saying "Everything they touch turns to gold." However, for the rest of us, it is a little more involved than that. It takes awareness, intention, and a little bit of preparation and planning. It also takes a clear vision for what we want to achieve or who we want to become. This isn't like another New Year's resolution that is bound to fail. This is more thoughtful, orchestrated, and planned. This week, we want you to **PREPARE TO LAUNCH**. We believe that anything is possible, but we also believe it takes a plan and a lot of work. Nothing meaningful in life comes easy. This week, discover what you want to launch in your life and for your family. Maybe you already know what it is because your family has already discussed your short- and long-term goals. Or maybe you need to come together to get more clarity on it by creating a vision board, setting your goals, and encouraging one another. It's time to get prepared to shoot for the moon by making a plan and believing you can get there. Preparing to launch matters.

TOMORROW BELONGS ONLY TO THE PEOPLE WHO PREPARE FOR IT TODAY.

—Malcolm X

TAKE ACTION

FOR YOUR COMMUNITY: Is there a greenbelt in your community that always collects trash? A public wall that is full of noncontracted graffiti? Or a dilapidated playground? Organize a day for you and your team to make the needed improvements. There is no one to wait for; be the change.

FOR YOUR FAMILY: Create a family vision board for something you want to accomplish or create together. It might be to build a tree house, grow a garden, or go on vacation. Pull out the photos and words to create the vision, then create and execute the steps to make it a reality.

FOR YOU: Ideas are just ideas—there are plenty of them. But what is an idea you have had, or still have, but never pursued or launched? Maybe writing a book? Starting an online store? Running a marathon? You know what's coming next...go be spectacular.

GO BIG

TAKE ACTION

FOR YOUR COMMUNITY: Throw a community block party. See who is willing to join in the fun and what they are willing to bring. You are going to need food, music, games, chairs, something to drink, and so on. If you all go big together, it just might become your first annual event.

FOR YOUR FAMILY: When is the last time you had a family reunion? Is this even something your family does? Go big and plan the biggest-ever family reunion. Get other families within your family to help organize and orchestrate the reunion. Including everyone is part of going big. Have fun.

FOR YOU: Set a big goal for yourself. Like even a crazy goal. Remember, the worst thing that can happen is that you fall a little short, but if the goal is big enough, you will still have accomplished something spec-tacular. This is what going big is all about.

> **PUT YOUR NAME ON SOMETHING. IT BETTER BE THE BEST...YOU ONLY GET ONE SHOT.**
>
> —George Foreman

"Go big or go home." It's easy to hear this statement and think it means we always have to get first place, be the number one person in charge, make the most money, own the biggest house on the block, and drive the nicest car on the market. If that's what you've always dreamed of achieving and you accomplished it, then that's awesome. But that isn't the only form of going big, as we all have different dreams, hopes, and goals. Regardless of what that saying means to you, this week, we want you to **GO BIG**. At the end of the day, we all only have one life to live, and that goes for each member of our families as well. This thought can be both scary and exciting at the same time, but let's focus on why it is so spectacular. For some of us, this means becoming a first-grade teacher or a college professor. For others, it might be to become the best mom or dad we can, a full-time volunteer for causes we care about, or an elected official. Anything is possible, and now is your time. Whatever you do, give it your all. This month, we've felt the wonder, owned our awesomeness, and prepared to launch. All you have left to do is go big. Going big matters.

MONDAY GETS ADVENTUROUS

How does it feel when you're curious? Is it fun, exciting, or scary? Possibly a combination of all three? While being curious can definitely be scary, it's a great way to live life. Approaching things with a new mindset and with the intention to learn is powerful, and it means we're never stuck in one place. This month is all about taking that curiosity to a new level by becoming more adventurous. Being adventurous might feel strange at first—especially if we're used to staying inside our comfort zones—but there is so much to discover in the world. It's time we get out of our family routines and the daily grind and see life as something to uncover and discover together every single day. Let's do things we have never done before. Let's open our eyes to new possibilities and ways we can help one another grow and stretch a little bit. The very act of starting and having a family might be one of the greatest adventures ever, so you are already prepared for anything that comes your way this month. Being adventurous matters.

THIS WEEK...
CONQUER A FEAR

For most of us, fears are a normal part of being alive. In some cases, our fears are falsely created in our heads, and the backronym "false evidence appearing real" is the perfect way to understand and overcome them. However, in other cases, our fears can be based on our past experiences. For example, a bite from a poisonous spider will keep you from wanting another one, or the broken trust of a friend might keep you from being vulnerable in future relationships. The challenge is that we can't go through life creating a laundry list of fears that shrink our world and keep us from experiencing everything life has to offer. So this week, it's time to **CONQUER A FEAR**. There is a good chance you or someone in your family has a fear to overcome. Maybe a fear of flying keeps you from seeing the world. Maybe a fear of being judged keeps you from speaking your truth. Maybe a fear of failing keeps you from trying new challenges. The next time you feel that desire to hesitate or stop or turn back, take a moment to ask yourself a simple question: what is the worst thing that can happen? If the answer isn't too bad, then take a second step, and then a third right toward it. Before you know it, you will have courageously overcome it. Conquering a fear matters.

TAKE ACTION

FOR YOUR COMMUNITY:
Families have fears that start outside their homes. Parents worry about the safety of their children. Children might be afraid of being bullied. Have an honest conversation about these fears, and work together to calm them. Everyone might need to be open to making a few adjustments.

FOR YOUR FAMILY: Play a game of "Who is afraid of what?" Let every family member share a fear that holds them back, then create a five-step plan to overcome each person's fear. If someone needs to go a little slower, then create a ten-step plan. Take each step together for each fear.

FOR YOU: Do you have a fear that keeps you from enjoying life more or achieving certain goals? What does it feel like to envision no longer having that fear? Can you feel it? Begin the process of overcoming this fear one small step at a time and once and for all.

EVERYTHING YOU'VE EVER WANTED IS ON THE OTHER SIDE OF FEAR.

—George Addair

83

THIS WEEK...
DECIDE TO DISCOVER

TAKE ACTION

FOR YOUR COMMUNITY: Go on a family field trip. Pack lunch, jump in the car or on public transportation, and hit the road. If you are feeling really adventurous, don't even plan it first. Just follow the signs or how you feel in the moment.

FOR YOUR FAMILY: Create a discovery dial. Draw a circle on a piece of paper with eight slices, so it looks like a pizza. Have family members fill in the slices with something they would like to discover. Each week, drop a penny onto the circle, and discover your family's new discovery mission.

FOR YOU: Do you know how to replace the brakes or change the oil in your car? How to make pico de gallo or sushi? What creates a breathtaking sunset or the perfect wave? How to sew? Decide to discover how something is done or created.

> **THE WORLD IS BIG, AND I WANT TO HAVE A GOOD LOOK AT IT BEFORE IT GETS DARK.**
>
> —John Muir

Human beings have always been focused on discovering. We've discovered cures for illnesses. We've discovered new cultures, languages, and galaxies. We've also discovered new forms of transportation, new underground cities, and new ways to better understand one another. And just when we think we have discovered everything there is to discover, we quickly learn that there is so much more work to be done. So this week, we want you to **DECIDE TO DISCOVER**. Every great discovery began with a decision—an intentional choice to learn or find something beyond our current understanding. Those decisions meant everything and stood in stark contrast to the common belief that we have experienced all there is to experience in life. Be honest: have you sometimes suffered from the "know-it-all" syndrome? Sometimes age has a way of bringing that out in us. Well, we hate to break the news, but no one knows it all. No one family knows it all either. There is so much to discover when we understand how much we don't know that we don't know. This is what makes life an adventure. So get excited about the new possibilities. Deciding to discover matters.

THIS WEEK...
CHANGE YOUR ROUTINE

How do you get to work every day? Where do you shop for groceries, clothes, or your dry cleaners? Who is in charge of what house chores? How does your family spend your weekends? We suspect these were pretty easy questions to answer. Why? Because we are creatures of habit, and we thrive with routines. There is nothing wrong with this, but it doesn't really align with our big push for adventure this month. So in the spirit of being adventurous, we want you to **CHANGE YOUR ROUTINE**. We created routines because they work for us. They take the thinking out of things, and we can do them on autopilot, often while doing something else at the same time. But let's have some fun. Maybe you can turn off the TV a half hour earlier to do some yoga in the evening because you're committing to being healthier. Maybe it's time to reinstate family dinners because you stopped sitting at the table together. Whatever it is, by changing how you live your life, you open yourself up to new ways of thinking, new people, and new discoveries all around. It's like giving your family a fresh start. This week, change things up and see what happens. Changing your routine matters.

IF YOU ALWAYS DO WHAT YOU'VE ALWAYS DONE, YOU ALWAYS GET WHAT YOU'VE ALWAYS GOTTEN.

—Jessie Potter

TAKE ACTION

FOR YOUR COMMUNITY: What is something in your community that your family has always wanted to do but hasn't made happen yet? Visit an animal sanctuary or a museum? Discover a new hiking trail? Try a new restaurant? Your community has so much to offer; go discover it together.

FOR YOUR FAMILY: Does your family have some routines that need to be changed up a bit? Allow each family member to identify one routine they think needs improvement, and then commit together to changing those routines. Teamwork makes the dream work. Enjoy your new and improved routines.

FOR YOU: Bad habits are just routines that don't serve us well—smoking, not being punctual, not sleeping enough, looking at our phones too much, not exercising, etc. Identify a bad habit, and let this be your inspiration to change your routine. Let's create more healthy routines in our lives.

THIS WEEK...
START A HOBBY

TAKE ACTION

FOR YOUR COMMUNITY: Do you have a hobby? Is it something you can share with other people? Can you teach a class on it? If so, invite people in your community to join and learn from you. Sharing skills is a great way to connect more with your community.

FOR YOUR FAMILY: As a family, play the Hobbies A to Z Game. Write down a hobby that starts with every letter of the alphabet. Once completed, find one that sparks everyone's interest and get started. Just remember that for it to become a hobby, this can't be one and done. Give it time.

FOR YOU: Is there a hobby you have always wanted to start but never have? Learn a new language? Learn a musical instrument? Learn how to paint? Starting today, just commit thirty minutes a week to it. No expectations. No judgment. Just enjoy the adventure.

A HOBBY A DAY KEEPS THE DOLDRUMS AWAY.

—Phyllis McGinley

Hobbies are delightful things. They build on our natural curiosity and bring excitement and joy into our lives in so many different ways. But this doesn't mean we are good at starting or sticking to them. We live busy lives, we have our routines, and sometimes it just feels like we don't have the time or the energy for one more thing. But this week, we are asking you to finish our month of being adventurous in strong fashion. We want you to **START A HOBBY**. The wonderful thing about hobbies is that they're habits and activities that are driven by our interests. They are a spark for creativity and have a way of bringing back our childlike, playful ways. Hobbies are also great places to build relationships and community. When you start a photography class, you find others who care about art and documenting life in an expressive way. When you join a book club, you're joining a community of people who are excited to investigate the world through literature. And if there is a hobby your entire family can do together, you just massively increased your quality time together. Sold yet? Good. Starting a hobby matters.

MONDAY GETS COMPASSIONATE

Compassion is one of the most beautiful acts of service. The willingness to be there for someone physically, mentally, or emotionally is as profound as it gets. We would like to believe that if people didn't have any other responsibilities or things to do, they would spend all their waking hours being compassionate for someone. But the truth is that just as much as we all would like to be compassion spreaders, there is a good chance we are all in need of a little compassion ourselves. We are exhausted and worn down, and our bowls are often pretty empty, especially when it comes to our families. As uplifting and life-giving as they can potentially be, they can also be overwhelming and exhausting at times. Let's commit to leading and living with more compassion. Because a world without it is a disaster. The same goes for a family. One filled with love, kindness, and compassion is a beautiful place and a beautiful family. It's the only way we can move forward as people. It's worth it. Being compassionate matters.

WALK IN THEIR SHOES

We are often quicker to judge than we are to understand. We even do it to ourselves. Instead of showing empathy or compassion, we pick ourselves apart for every imperfection. Our hope is that you will start to take a different approach. Instead of choosing judgment, choose curiosity, because curiosity is the first step toward understanding others. Instead of placing expectations on your family members, place encouragement. Instead of placing performance pressure, place pride in their effort. This week, we want you to **WALK IN THEIR SHOES**. This week, try understanding what a day, a month, or even a year of someone else's life is like. Yes, even for your spouse or your children. Have you ever sincerely imagined what they think and feel on a daily basis? Just because we live our life one way, it doesn't mean it's the "right" or "only" way to live. Just because one generation did it one way, it doesn't mean the next generation is supposed to follow. So try to compassionately understand why people, including your family members, make different choices. Once you do this, things might change forever—for you, your family, and your community. Walking in their shoes matters.

TAKE ACTION

FOR YOUR COMMUNITY: As a family, volunteer at a senior living facility. Senior living facilities are filled with beautiful people and stories. There also happen to be a lot of people who would love a visit and to feel like they matter. Get ready to listen and learn a ton about life.

FOR YOUR FAMILY: We often live in silos, even within our own families. Host a family lunch and learn. Let everyone know they will have five to ten minutes to give a presentation on something that matters to them or that they have been focused on, thinking about, or feeling.

FOR YOU: If we are honest, having judgments of others is something with which we all struggle. Do you have a precon-ceived notion or a conscious or unconscious bias? It's time to open your mind and heart, to lean in, and to learn, all in the spirit of personal growth and compas-sion.

THE GREAT GIFT OF HUMAN BEINGS IS THAT WE HAVE THE POWER OF EMPATHY.

— Meryl Streep

THIS WEEK...
RIGHT A WRONG

TAKE ACTION

FOR YOUR COMMUNITY: Mistakes can be followed up by criticism, disdain, or resentment. Or they can be followed up by understanding and love. What is your family's mistake policy? How can it be more compassionate? Work together. You just might right a wrong policy in the process.

FOR YOUR FAMILY: Host an open mic night. Allow each family member to share an experience where they felt wronged by a family member or when they wronged a family member themselves. No arguing. No interrupting. The only follow-up should be, "I'm so sorry. I love you and really appreciate you sharing."

FOR YOU: Are you good at taking ownership of your mistakes? It's okay if the answer is no, but now ask yourself why, because identifying and unpacking that answer is your key to righting-a-wrong freedom. You will soon discover the healing power of "I'm sorry."

IF YOU'RE AFRAID OF BEING LONELY, DON'T TRY TO BE RIGHT.

—Jules Renard

It's unavoidable: hurting someone else, offending them, or bothering them in some way. We're human after all. No one is perfect. But as much as these statements are true, it's important not to use them as excuses. Each of us has an impact on others, and it's up to us to understand what kind of impact we have, then to commit to making the most positive impact possible. And when we have a misstep, it's up to us to **RIGHT A WRONG**. Shockingly, there is a term to describe people who don't like to apologize: non-apologists. A non-apologist would rather not apologize and feel guilty about their actions, because apologizing would open the door to shame, which would make them feel bad about themselves. Sorry, non-apologists, we aren't buying it, because we know you expect apologies from those who have wronged you. Don't you? It's time for all of us to practice saying those two powerful words— "I'm sorry"—and go one step further to make things right. A family that can't apologize will have a difficult time connecting and building deeper bonds. If everyone is focused on being right, there is no room for kindness. Without kindness, there is no compassion. We think you get where this is going. Get excited, because righting our wrongs matters.

BUILD BRIDGES

Compassion is rooted in the desire to want to connect. It says, "I see you," or at least, "I'm trying to see you." It also says, "I want to grow closer, not drift further apart." It is an outreached hand, and it takes courage, but it is the only way we grow closer as family members and as a world. This week, we want you to **BUILD BRIDGES**. Bridges are beautiful things. They take us from one side of a situation to another. They're places where people can meet halfway, both literally and figuratively. They're essential for relationships to exist and thrive. This week, we're asking you to be courageous and find ways to build bridges in your family. Find ways to connect with others who mean the world to you. Invest in building bridges in your life instead of building walls around yourself, your family, or people in your community who might be "different" from you. Extend a hand to those who need help, to those who might have wronged you, and even to total strangers. This week, bring understanding, respect, and care to the relationships in your life, and commit to building bridges. We will all benefit greatly from a world with more bridges and fewer walls. Building bridges matters.

MEN BUILD TOO MANY WALLS AND NOT ENOUGH BRIDGES.

—Georges Pire

TAKE ACTION

FOR YOUR COMMUNITY:
Sadly, our communities are filled with walls. These might not be actual physical walls, but their presence is absolutely felt. As a family, commit to building bridges in your community. And where there are walls, start to chip away at them.

FOR YOUR FAMILY: Is your family filled with bridge builders or wall builders? Tough question, isn't it? The next time it feels like walls are building in your family, be the one who lovingly knocks them down. And make sure everyone knows they have the same hammer in hand.

FOR YOU: When something doesn't go your way, how do you react? When a disagreement surfaces in your family or with a friend, what is your response? Do you build walls and disengage or do you build a bridge and lean in with love? Be the one who builds the bridge.

THIS WEEK...
LISTEN UP

TAKE ACTION

FOR YOUR COMMUNITY:
Gossip destroys communities. If you ever find yourself in a gossipy conversation, simply let the gossipers know you are not really comfortable with the current conversation. This might sound harsh to do, but it is actually a powerful act of love and compassion for everyone. You will see.

FOR YOUR FAMILY: Interrupting someone is one of the fastest ways to communicate that what they have to say isn't important. Does your family tend to interrupt, or do you listen lovingly? Time for a change. And saying, "I'm sorry for interrupting" but continuing to talk is not one of the new rules.

FOR YOU: Are you a listener or a fixer? This week, just listen. Don't feel the need to fix a single thing.

> **THE FIRST DUTY OF LOVE IS TO LISTEN.**
>
> —Paul Tillich

As complicated as we are as human beings, we are also pretty simple. We all have basic needs—a roof over our heads, shoes on our feet, food, water, and safety. In addition to these survival needs, we also have human needs, or needs of the heart. We crave a sense of belonging, healthy relationships, love, purpose, and significance. We want to know that we matter. There are endless things we can do to help one another feel more like we matter, and this week, we're featuring one of the easiest and most effective methods. It's time for all of us to **LISTEN UP**. Feeling heard is everything. It lets us know our thoughts and feelings matter. It helps us understand we have something of value to share with the world and reminds us that someone truly cares about us. Why? Because they took the time to truly listen—not just for the sake of listening but for the desire to understand. We know the impact of being listened to and importance of being heard, so let's gift it to as many people as we can this week and beyond. Listening shows you care. It says, "You matter." It is an act of love and compassion. So give it freely. Listening up matters.

MONDAY GETS GRATEFUL

Being thankful has many layers to it. There are those things in life we often take for granted yet bring us incredible internal joy. It could be an annual birthday phone call from a relative, a neighbor always greeting you on your walk, or the way your parent or significant other makes your lunch. Then there are the times when people thank us for something we have done and we get to wrestle with actually accepting and embracing their gratitude. Finally, there are those times when we get to give thanks and express gratitude to someone else. Expressing gratitude, even for the smallest acts, takes time, thoughtfulness, and sometimes a bit of bravery. And when we are all more open to feel, receive, and give thanks, we are able to create a "pay it forward" dynamic that can spread like wildfire. So let's commit to feeling, receiving, and expressing gratitude like never before. Just watch what happens. Being grateful matters.

THIS WEEK...
GIVE GRATITUDE

They say actions speak louder than words. In other words, how we give gratitude matters. Have you ever received a thank-you note or greeting that felt empty and wasn't sincere? Or have you ever casually said "thanks" to someone and whisked away, when a proper "thank you" and taking the time to make sure it landed in a genuine manner would have been more appropriate? Similarly, have you ever asked someone how they are doing but didn't really hear or act like you cared about their response? How we express ourselves matters, as does showing appreciation. So this week, we want you to genuinely **GIVE GRATITUDE**. This doesn't have to be an extravagant show of emotions or an elaborate gift or gesture; it simply needs to be genuine and from the heart. Giving gratitude doesn't even have to cost anything—a handwritten note can go a long way. A sincere showing of appreciation lets someone know how much they matter to you, and we think that is pretty important stuff. This week, it's up to us to take the opportunity to give gratitude. Let's understand and connect to that fulfilling feeling. Giving and feeling grateful connects us to one another. Families feed from it. Giving gratitude matters.

> **FEELING GRATITUDE AND NOT EXPRESSING IT IS LIKE WRAPPING A PRESENT AND NOT GIVING IT.**
>
> —William Arthur Ward

TAKE ACTION

FOR YOUR COMMUNITY: Think of an unsung hero in your community. Typically, these are people who serve us each and every day but easily go invisible. Figure out a meaningful gift or gesture you can share with them to let them know how grateful you are for their service.

FOR YOUR FAMILY: One of the biggest reasons people don't write thank-you notes is because they don't have stationery. First, purchase a box of thank-you notes. Second, establish a twenty-four-hour rule, whereby each family member has twenty-four hours after receiving any kind gesture to write a thank-you card.

FOR YOU: Make gratitude a daily practice. Either journal about it, meditate on it, or outwardly express at least one thing for which you are grateful every day.

THIS WEEK...
LOVE THE LITTLE THINGS

TAKE ACTION

FOR YOUR COMMUNITY: As a family, create a travel brochure for your community. Think about all the little things your community has to offer, add some pithy language and a few photos, and you are ready to attract tourists. Consider sharing your brochure with others to help spread the word.

FOR YOUR FAMILY: Create a gratitude jar. Grab a jar or shoebox, decorate it with messages or images of gratitude, and provide slips of paper and a pen. Ask each family member to write something about the family for which they are grateful. At the end of each week, read one slip together.

FOR YOU: Make it a daily practice to notice one new little thing every day and simply say "thank you" quietly to yourself while you enjoy it.

ENJOY THE LITTLE THINGS, FOR ONE DAY YOU MAY LOOK BACK AND REALIZE THEY WERE THE BIG THINGS.

—Robert Brault

It's easy to love the big things, like going on vacation, getting a new car, or seeing that delivery box on your front porch. But what about the small things? Do we spend enough time being grateful for those little moments and those tiny gestures that surround us each and every day? Chances are we don't, and we let our busyness get in the way. But not this week, because we are going to take the time to **LOVE THE LITTLE THINGS** and be super grateful for them. When we're grateful for the little things, it's almost like we're practicing being grateful for those bigger things in life, so we can really feel them when they happen to us. When we're actively grateful for the little things, we're balancing out our negativity bias or our tendency to see things in a negative light. We start to see that our lives and the world around us are really quite wonderful and full of goodness. There is so much to be grateful for; we just need to take better notice. So this week, if someone asks you, "How was your day?" instead of trying to find something big and awesome to tell them, focus on the little things, like noticing the fall leaves, sipping your first cup of coffee in the morning, feeling your pet's love, or hearing a great song in your car. See, loving the little things matters.

THIS WEEK…
GIVE ONE, GIVE ONE

We have all heard the marketing slogans "Buy one, give one" and "Buy one, get one." Maybe you have purchased a few products because one of these campaigns worked its magic on you. We are not here to judge, because either someone else benefited from your purchase or you got a real deal by getting two for the price of one. Nice work. But we have a new slogan for you we believe is more powerful and will create even more joy in the world. This week, we are asking you to **GIVE ONE, GIVE ONE**. There are a few things about this that we hope you love. First off, you don't have to buy anything. See, we are already saving you money! Second, however, we are asking you to give something and then give again. Maybe you have some well-cared-for clothing in your closet. Maybe you have an extra computer or a bunch of books you have already read. Or maybe you have an extra hour you can donate to a worthy cause. Of course, you will feel great joy in doing any of the above, but this is about creating joy for others. Think about the person on the receiving end of your generosity. Think about the life you are changing. All we need to do is give. No more buying, no more getting, only giving. Giving matters.

YOU CAN ALWAYS—ALWAYS—GIVE SOMETHING, EVEN IF IT'S A SIMPLE ACT OF KINDNESS.

—Anne Frank

TAKE ACTION

FOR YOUR COMMUNITY: Start a canned food drive in your neighborhood. In promoting it, make sure to communicate your goal, the time frame, how their cans will be collected or dropped off, and who the beneficiary of their generosity will be. And of course, when it is all over, make sure you express gratitude.

FOR YOUR FAMILY: Make family coupon books filled with things you are each willing to give to one another. For example: wash your car, do one load of your laundry, or cook dinner. Each week, allow one family member to pull one coupon from someone's coupon book. Have fun giving to one another.

FOR YOU Give one thing every day this week. You can give a smile to a stranger, a phone call to an old friend, clothing to a shelter, food to a food pantry, or time to a local cause. The choices are endless. Just give, and give again.

107

WAVER NO MORE

TAKE ACTION

FOR YOUR COMMUNITY: Every team needs someone who never wavers on finding the silver lining and helping others see the positive. Are you that person? If so, what do you do to help the team keep from wavering? If not, what can you do to become more of an unwavering force?

FOR YOUR FAMILY: Instead of teaching your children how to say thank you or calling them out when they don't say it, focus on teaching them how to be grateful. Just watch: they will always say thank you, because it comes from their authentic selves. Voilà!

FOR YOU: Think of a tough moment you experienced recently. Now ask yourself, "What was I supposed to learn from that?" What comes up for you? Does it shift how you view that experience? Does it possibly make you just a little grateful for it now? Great. That's a start.

> **YOU CAN'T STOP THE WAVES BUT YOU CAN LEARN TO SURF.**
>
> —Jon Kabat-Zinn

It is easy to be grateful when everything is going well, much like it is easy to be nice to someone when they are being nice to you. But gratitude can't be something we turn on and turn off. We are either grateful or we are not. It's the same as unconditional love. But this doesn't mean it's easy, especially when someone wrongs us or when life throws us challenges. Where and how do we find gratitude in those moments? We want to give it a shot, so this week, we want you to **WAVER NO MORE**. There is a question we can ask ourselves when something doesn't go well: "What am I supposed to learn from this?" We can apply it to losing a job or even a loved one. We can ask ourselves this question if we get into a car accident or forget to call a family member on their birthday. The reason this question is so powerful is that it removes us from the victim position and immediately thrusts us into a place of growth and progress. This question helps us see how we can see, think, or act differently with the goal of becoming better, healthier, and more aware. For this, we should be forever grateful, for we now know how to find the good in every bad. Never wavering matters.

MONDAY GETS EMPOWERED

We all want to live life to the fullest. We want to do the things we want to do and dream the dreams we want to dream. We often look to other people for that empowerment, and less often, we realize that we have the power and strength in us already. This month, we are going to get supercharged to learn, grow, achieve, and get after it. Before we get started, however, let's take a moment to envision that reality. Close your eyes and think about a person named Empowered. Maybe Empowered is you. What actions does Empowered take? How does Empowered carry themselves? What words does Empowered say? Does Empowered operate with purpose and determination? Do they ever fail...and then get back up? Does Empowered celebrate the small wins along the way? Now open your eyes and see yourself as Empowered. Can you feel it? Awesome. Just remember that being empowered isn't about creating a single inspirational moment—it's about raising the bar for how you live your life. Start today. You have everything you need. Getting empowered matters.

THIS WEEK...
CONNECT TO PURPOSE

The word *why* might be just a few letters, but it has played a significant role in humanity. The Greek philosopher Socrates, responsible for the Socratic method, taught us how to get to the bottom of things through a series of why questions. If you have young children, you certainly know their love affair with the word *why*. Understanding our why is the same as understanding our purpose…the reason we exist. This is big stuff. So this week, we want you to **CONNECT TO PURPOSE**. Being completely in touch with why you exist is heavy, but we also think it is exhilarating and empowering. It starts with undoubtedly knowing there is nothing accidental about your existence, rather that your life matters for something pretty special. It starts with developing a personal mission statement for your life. It starts with deeply connecting with what matters most to you and being crystal clear on how you want to spend your time. Doesn't that feel good already? We hope so. It's time to step out of going through the motions. It's time to get to know yourself, your passions, and your purpose. Connecting to purpose matters.

FIND OUT WHO YOU ARE AND DO IT ON PURPOSE.

—Dolly Parton

TAKE ACTION

FOR YOUR COMMUNITY: Every community is built on values; so is purpose. What communities are you a part of—friendships, family, school, team, or work— and what values drive their purpose? How you can play a bigger role in making sure your communities are connecting to their purpose?

FOR YOUR FAMILY: As a family, come to an agreement on five words that perfectly describe each family member. Once each person has their five words, have a discussion about how these five words might be the foundation for their life purpose.

FOR YOU: Take a moment to answer to these three questions: What are my intrinsic strengths? What interests do I want to explore? What can I contribute to the world? Congratulations on getting one major step closer to defining your purpose.

113

THIS WEEK...
BE TENACIOUS

TAKE ACTION

FOR YOUR COMMUNITY: Is there something about your community that you have always wanted to see improve? Maybe it is getting people to drive slower down your street. Maybe it is getting people to stop littering in your local park. Take charge. Be tenacious. Yes, you can help solve these issues.

FOR YOUR FAMILY: Create a mini goal for your family, something you can do in a month. Together, determine twelve mini goals that you can accomplish as a unit. By the end of a year, you will have achieved twelve new goals together. That's one empowered year.

FOR YOU: What is something big you have always wanted to go after in life but never quite got there? Maybe you never even tried for it. Or maybe you started the pursuit of it but something got in your way. Now's the time. Be fierce. Be tenacious.

> YOU NEED TO BELIEVE IN YOURSELF AND WHAT YOU DO. BE TENACIOUS AND GENUINE.
>
> —Christian Louboutin

Tenacity is a trait—and a skill—that's important to each and every one of us. Tenacity is also a choice and something we can get better at over time as we learn to take a stand for what we believe in or pursue our passions. How tenacious are you? How determined, tireless, and persistent are you when it comes to something that means a lot to you? This week, it's time to **BE TENACIOUS** and not give up on whatever it is you are pursuing. Maybe it is a positive change you want for your family. Maybe it is a new hobby or a beneficial health goal. Whatever it is, just know that it will take courage to follow through and believe in yourself, especially if others (or the world) are telling you that you shouldn't even try. It will cause you to ask how much you really want this thing, how much it really means to you. This is where our actions speak louder than our words or even ideas. Take this week to go for it and never quit. Being tenacious matters.

Very few people set out with the goal of failing. We all want success…instantly. But the truth is that we will all fail at something at some point in our lives. Actually, we will fail several times, and there is absolutely nothing wrong with that. Doesn't that feel good to know and embrace? Doesn't that already take the pressure off? Many of us are taught or think that perfection is everything, but in reality, perfection is exhausting, and there is no such thing. It's also inevitably frustrating and just not a necessary goal. This week, we want you to remember that failure is an option and to **GET BACK UP**. Fearing failure can keep us from trying. It steals our power and our willingness to be empowered and go for our dreams. However, failing is part of life, and it's something we can use to grow. But it's okay to feel it when it happens. It's healthy to feel the disappointment, sadness, or whatever emotion it surfaces for you. But then lift your chin, and take your next step forward in life. Show yourself—and others—that you're powerful enough to keep going. Getting back up matters.

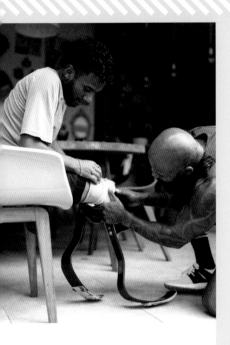

YOU JUST CAN'T BEAT THE PERSON WHO NEVER GIVES UP.

—Babe Ruth

TAKE ACTION

FOR YOUR COMMUNITY: We are all aware of the fact that disasters strike. They can be in the form of a virus, a hurricane or tornado, devastating fires, or crime and vandalism. When disaster strikes your community, be one of the empowered ones who helps it get back up.

FOR YOUR FAMILY: Establish a "fail forward" policy in your family. This policy celebrates taking a risk, shooting for the moon, and trying new things, even if we fall short or stumble along the way. Make sure everyone knows that failing forward will *always* be celebrated.

FOR YOU: Pull out a piece of paper and a pen and write a personal thank-you note to failure: "Dear Failure…" Remember this is a thank-you note, and make sure that failure knows how much you appreciate it and why. Don't feel silly; just start writing.

THIS WEEK...
CELEBRATE THE EFFORT

TAKE ACTION

FOR YOUR COMMUNITY: Throw a celebration for any community you are part of. Things to consider: How will you celebrate? What will the celebration include? When will you do it? Your celebration will inspire other celebrations, and that too is worth celebrating.

FOR YOUR FAMILY: Encourage each family member to pick either one family success or one family failure, and then bake a cake to represent or symbolize those incidents. Once it's ready, add a candle for each incident, then blow them out and enjoy the cake, all in the spirit of progress and effort.

FOR YOU: Think of a recent time when you truly gave your best effort at something. What was it? How did it feel? Regardless of the outcome, it's time to celebrate it. You pick how to celebrate; just make sure you do.

> **CELEBRATE EVERY SUCCESS, BUT DON'T FORGET TO ENJOY THOSE SCARS OF FAILURES.**
>
> —Debasish Mridha

Being empowered doesn't just happen overnight. It's a lifelong commitment that takes work and dedication. You may experience seasons when being empowered just feels easier and more natural than other times. You may hit several speed bumps along the path that slow your progress, but you will also experience several wins that propel you forward. In our opinion, both persevering through the setbacks and embracing the victories—big and small—deserve to be celebrated. So this week, we want you to take time to **CELEBRATE THE EFFORT**. Don't let the world define your steps as successes or failures; just see them as steps to whatever comes next. Commit to learning from and celebrating whatever happens on your journey, and practice being grateful for all of it. When we do this, not only does it guard us from having a victim mentality, it actually empowers and inspires us to continue moving forward, knowing that we are better off with having put in an effort. So from this day forward, choose to celebrate, even when it doesn't go perfectly. Celebrating the effort matters.

MONDAY GETS HOPEFUL

It's often said that when all else fails, we always have hope. But is that how we really want to accept the idea of hope? That it's the last thing remaining after every other option has failed? In some sense, that might be true, but this idea completely ignores the true importance and power of hope. Because hope isn't last—it's first. Hope is the thing that gets us out of bed in the morning. Hope is the thing that inspires us and makes us believe that anything is possible. When we were young, we hoped to be astronauts, firefighters, doctors, professional athletes, and this hope was what drove us to believe we could do it. Our hopes were limitless and abundant. But what about now? What does hope mean to you? What does hope feel and look like to you? Is hope still alive and well in you and your family? Let's surround ourselves and our families with pathways that create hope. Let's be unapologetic and limitless with our hope. It's time for all of us to be more hopeful and to always hope for the best. Being hopeful matters.

LIGHT UP THE ROOM

The only way to diminish darkness is to add light. And what creates that light? Hope. Hope is the spark that allows light to permeate the gloom. It's the stars glittering in the midnight sky. It's the light at the end of the tunnel, the sun rising in the morning sky or pushing through the clouds to create silver linings. You are also the light, so this week, we want you to **LIGHT UP THE ROOM**. At the very core of knowing how much you matter is the idea that you are powerful beyond your wildest imagination. Every thought you have, every action you take, and every word you utter has an impact on the world around you. You impact every relationship you are in, every room you walk into, and even every stranger you encounter. This is exciting but also overwhelming, because it forces us to make a choice. Will our actions, words, and thoughts bring light or darkness to the world? It's that simple. In every moment of every day, we get to make this choice. So what kind of family do you want to be? We hope your answer touches on words like *loving*, *kind*, *caring*, *uplifting*, *joyful*, and *generous*. In which case, this week is perfect for you and your family, because it allows you to be the light. Shine bright. Lighting up the room matters.

**IF YOU HAVE NO
SHADOWS THEN
YOU'RE NOT STANDING
IN THE LIGHT.**

—Lady Gaga

TAKE ACTION

FOR YOUR COMMUNITY: Think about someone in your community who positively impacts others and lights up the room, possibly a friend, coworker, teacher, or elected official. Take the time to write them a handwritten letter to express how much you appreciate their being. It will certainly light them up even more.

FOR YOUR FAMILY: Every person in your family has a unique superpower that only they can bring to your family. Help everyone identify their superpower, and reinforce how important it is for them to use it in a way that brings light and hope to your family.

FOR YOU: What are some simple, powerful things you do to light up the room? Maybe it is something you do when you first walk into work or your home? Create a list of more ways you can light up the room wherever you are. Consider asking your family for input.

THIS WEEK...
PRACTICE POSITIVITY

TAKE ACTION

FOR YOUR COMMUNITY: We help establish the climate of our community. How do you react when someone cuts you off on the road? When someone is being rude to someone else? If it is typically negative, consider what a positive response might be and the impact that could have instead.

FOR YOUR FAMILY: Make a master list using chart paper. On the left side, list common negative words you might have heard around the house. On the right side, list positive alternatives for each of the negatives. Encourage one another to stick with the right side of the chart from this day forward.

FOR YOU: Think about one positive thought you are willing to have all week long. Call it your mantra for the week. Do you have it? Great, now commit to practicing positivity with it all week long.

SO MANY OF OUR DREAMS AT FIRST SEEM IMPOSSIBLE. AND THEN THEY SEEM IMPROBABLE. AND THEN WHEN WE SUMMON THE WILL, THEY SOON BECOME INEVITABLE.

—Christopher Reeve

As much as we like to pride ourselves on being upbeat, positive, and optimistic people, it is a strange truth that bad news seems to spread quicker than good news. There is also a reason the evening news rarely allocates time for uplifting and inspiring news stories and that most of our popular television shows aren't what one might call "feel good TV." Throw in some of the negativity and bullying that takes place online and on social media, and it is no wonder why sometimes things just don't feel so great. Well, in the spirit of being hopeful, it's time to **PRACTICE POSITIVITY**. It's very easy to slip and see the negative instead of celebrating the positive. It's also easy to see the ugliness and imperfections instead of being astonished by the beauty. But we can change our ways, and there is a reason we chose the word *practice*: because remaining focused on the positive in ourselves, in our families, and in our world just might take practice—a true concerted and unwavering effort. But we need it, both individually and collectively, so let's be powerful positivity professionals. Let's lift one another up. Let's play and laugh. Let's take notice of the beauty in and around us. Let's be the legion of positivity, because practicing positivity matters.

START A LEGACY

The idea of leaving a legacy has an interesting way of placing it as something that happens sometime in the distant future. In other words, we don't need to worry about our legacy today. But this couldn't be further from the truth, because we create our legacies starting now. Architects create structural legacies, like the Eiffel Tower. Artists create creative legacies, like the *Mona Lisa*. These legacies took time. They didn't happen overnight. So what about you? What is your legacy going to be? What about your family's legacy? If you haven't thought much about it, then you're going to love this week. It's time to **START A LEGACY**. To achieve this, it's often easiest to start with the end in mind. In other words, how do you want to be remembered? To put it in a more hopeful light, if you were to ask anyone who knows you or your family well to choose ten words to describe you, what do you hope they would say? Do you have a pretty clear idea? Perfect. Now commit the rest of your life to being *that* person or *that* family. If you hope they say "creative," then go create something tangible that will last forever. If you hope they say "kind," then do something kind for someone every day. Enjoy the journey. Starting a legacy matters.

THE TRUE MEANING OF LIFE IS TO PLANT TREES, UNDER WHOSE SHADE YOU DO NOT EXPECT TO SIT.

— Nelson Henderson

TAKE ACTION

FOR YOUR COMMUNITY: Every city has a motto. They are often put on signs on the freeway or archways downtown. What is your community's motto, and how well is it living up to it? If not well, consider ways you and your family can get involved to create more alignment.

FOR YOUR FAMILY: Come up with ten words you would hope other people or families use to describe your family. Once you have your words, do a quick family check-in to see if you are living in a manner consistent with that legacy. If not, create a plan to clean things up.

FOR YOU: Today is the first day of your new and revitalized commitment to creating your legacy. Write a paragraph or two about what you envision for your legacy. Then write down real action steps you can take to start living your legacy today. Remember, it starts with you. You matter.

THIS WEEK...
BELIEVE IT'S POSSIBLE

TAKE ACTION

FOR YOUR COMMUNITY: As a family, pick one important thing you all believe is possible to create or achieve together that benefits your community. Give it a time frame, create a plan to achieve it, and of course, celebrate your accomplishment when the time is right. Remember, it only happened because you believed.

FOR YOUR FAMILY: As a family, write family mission and vision statements together. The mission statement focuses on your values and goals as a family. The vision statement clarifies your long-term vision and hope. Once you have written them, empower everyone to live by them as well.

FOR YOU: Where in your life can you shift the paradigm of "impossible" into "I'm possible"? Maybe it's something you, your spouse, or your family that you had lost hope in? Impossible is so *meh*. From this day on, you only know "I'm possible."

> **NOTHING IS IMPOSSIBLE. THE WORD ITSELF SAYS, "I'M POSSIBLE."**
>
> —Audrey Hepburn

There is a fine line between hope and belief. It's almost as if they require a little bit of a reality check…but not too much of one. For example, hoping that millions of dollars will fall from the sky might not be so realistic. Or hoping that you can run a sub-two-hour marathon might seem a little unbelievable. However, this is not to say that hoping to be successful or a superfast runner is a bad thing. So with a subtle reality check yet beyond what we typically think is possible, this week, we want you to **BELIEVE IT'S POSSIBLE**. What is something you have always wanted to do or achieve? What is something you hoped for, for yourself or for your family? Do you still believe these dreams are possible, or have you let the negative self-talk and the naysayers squash your beliefs? In other words, have you settled into acceptance and status quo instead of keeping the fire burning? What would it take to believe again? How can you rally your troops to be a family that believes again? You have heard it before: "impossible" is just "I'm possible." And of course, we know that "extraordinary" is just "extra ordinary." So you decide. Do you want to be "possible" or "extra"? Go for it. Believing it's possible matters.

FAMILY DINNER
CONVERSATION
STARTERS

MONDAY GETS FUN

GET GOOFY 2
What is the goofiest thing you have ever done?

LEND A HAND 4
When is the last time you accomplished something with someone else? How do you think it would have felt different or not as much fun if you had accomplished it on your own?

SURPRISE SOMEONE 6
Why do you think surprises are so much fun?

SPICE IT UP 8
Would you rather have to eat the same food for every meal for the rest of your life or have to eat something different for every meal for the rest of your life? Why?

MONDAY GETS ACCEPTING

EMBRACE UNIQUENESS 12
What is something you used to hope was different about yourself but now you see it as unique and are grateful for it?

CELEBRATE CHANGE 14
Why do you think change is so hard for people to accept?

KNOW WHAT MATTERS MOST   16

What is on your list of what matters most to you, and how do you make sure you give enough attention to those things?

ASK FOR INPUT   18

Do you like getting feedback from people? Why or why not?

MONDAY GETS CONSISTENT

BE PATIENT   22

Would you rather hurry through something to get it done quickly, even if it means not performing as well, or would you rather take your time in order to get it right? Can you think of an example of this in your life?

PUT IN THE WORK   24

What do you think about the statement "If you love what you are doing, then it is never work"?

BELIEVE IN BOUNDARIES   26

What is a personal boundary that you wished people honored more?

HONOR YOUR WORD   28

Do you believe that words matter? Why or why not?

MONDAY GETS HEALTHY

TAKE OWNERSHIP 32

What can you do to become a healthier person? Are you ready to take ownership of it?

PRACTICE PEACE 34

Is it easy for you to sit still and be quiet? If not, why do you think that is the case?

CHECK YOUR CHOICES 36

How much would someone have to pay you to take away the least healthy food you like to eat for the rest of your life?

FEEL THE FEELS 38

What is an emotion that you love to feel? Why? What is an emotion that you don't like to feel? Why?

MONDAY GETS LOVING

ASK QUESTIONS 42

What is the most meaningful question someone has ever asked you? What is the most meaningful question you have ever asked?

MAKE TIME 44

If you had an extra hour every day, how would you use it to do something loving for yourself or for someone else?

CURATE COMPASSION   46

What does having compassion for someone or something mean to you?

CHOOSE KINDNESS   48

Do you believe that kindness is random, like random acts of kindness, or that it is planned?

MONDAY GETS MINDFUL

ENJOY THE NOW   52

What are things we can do as a family to be more present and to slow our roll to enjoy life more?

BE INTENTIONAL   54

If you had one wish for the world, what would it be? Why?

UNPLUG TO PLUG IN   56

Would you rather give up all electronics for a day or not eat for a day? Would you rather give up all electronics for a week or eat a cricket burrito?

SIMPLIFY YOUR LIFE   58

What is one thing that you can get rid of, cut from your schedule, or say no to this week to simplify your life?

MONDAY GETS CONNECTED

MAKE A MEMORY 62

What is one of your favorite family memories? What made it so special for you?

OPEN THE DOOR 64

On a scale of one to ten, with ten being high, how would you rate our family's communication skills? And what ideas might you have to improve it?

VALUE TRADITION 66

What is a new family tradition you think we should start?

GO WITH GRACE 68

Why do you think it is so challenging for people to forgive someone even though they also want to be forgiven by others?

MONDAY GETS SPECTACULAR

FEEL THE WONDER 72

What is something spectacular that happened to you today or in the past week, and how did it help you feel the wonder of life?

OWN YOUR AWESOMENESS 74

If you could have one awesome superpower, what would it be and why?

PREPARE TO LAUNCH 76

If you were given the funding to start a new business or create a new product or service, what would you launch?

GO BIG 78

What force do you think is more powerful, the desire to go big and win or the fear of failure and losing?

MONDAY GETS ADVENTUROUS

CONQUER A FEAR 82

How do our fears help or hurt us? What is your greatest fear? Why?

DECIDE TO DISCOVER 84

What do you think is the greatest invention or discovery ever? Why?

CHANGE YOUR ROUTINE 86

How hard would it be for you to eat with the opposite hand? Ready to switch your knife and fork and find out right now?

START A HOBBY 88

If you could master a new hobby or skill, what hobby or skill would you pick?

MONDAY GETS COMPASSIONATE

WALK IN THEIR SHOES   92

If you had to spend twenty-four hours homeless, in prison, or in a new country where no one understands you, which would you pick and why?

RIGHT A WRONG   94

Why do you think it so difficult for people to say, "I'm sorry"?

BUILD BRIDGES   96

How can you do a better job of building bridges with people who are different from you?

LISTEN UP   98

What is active listening, and why is it so important?

MONDAY GETS GRATEFUL

GIVE GRATITUDE   102

What are you most grateful for right now?

LOVE THE LITTLE THINGS   104

Why is it so important to notice and be grateful for the little things?

GIVE ONE, GIVE ONE   106

If you could end one global dilemma, which one would it be?

WAVER NO MORE   108

Where did the saying "Find the silver lining" originate, and what does it mean?

MONDAY GETS EMPOWERED

CONNECT TO PURPOSE   112

How would you explain the idea of living with purpose?

BE TENACIOUS   114

Is it better to work hard or to work smart? Or both?

GET BACK UP   116

When is a time when you got knocked down but got back up and tried again? What did you learn from the experience?

CELEBRATE THE EFFORT   118

There is a common proverb that says, "Life is a journey, not a destination." What does this statement mean to you, and how might it change your perspective?

MONDAY GETS HOPEFUL

LIGHT UP THE ROOM 122

What are common traits that people who light up the room possess? Do you think that these can be learned or that they are just born with them?

PRACTICE POSITIVITY 124

Do you think social media is good for people and the world, or does it have more of a negative impact on everything?

START A LEGACY 126

If you were given a lifetime achievement award, what achievement of yours would you like it to recognize? Keep in mind, this doesn't have to be anything you've done; it can also be for the type of person you are.

BELIEVE IT'S POSSIBLE 128

If you could wave your magic wand or see into a crystal ball, what is something that might seem impossible today that you hope or believe will become a reality in the future?

ABOUT THE AUTHOR

Matthew Emerzian is founder and chief inspiration officer of Every Monday Matters (EMM), a nonprofit organization committed to helping people and organizations understand how much and why they matter. Inspired by his book of the same name, EMM's programs have been utilized by some of America's largest corporations and more than two million students in forty-nine states and seven countries. His work has been hailed by publications such as *Fast Company*, *Huffington Post*, and Oprah.com, including his original bestselling title *Every Monday Matters*, which was featured on the *Today Show* and *Home and Family*. Over the past ten years, Emerzian has traveled the country sharing his unique story and insight on finding purpose. His life-changing message focuses on sustained personal and social change that happens by stepping outside ourselves by serving and connecting with one another. Emerzian has authored two other books, *Every Monday Matters: How to Kick Your Week Off with Passion, Purpose, and Positivity* (2019) and *You Matter: Learning to Love Who You Really Are* (2020). Emerzian holds a master's degree from the Anderson School of Management at UCLA and resides with his wife, Patty Malcolm, and their animals, Romy, Rooster, Rocky, and Rambo, in Sherman Oaks, California.

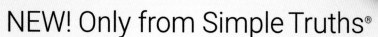

NEW! Only from Simple Truths®

IGNITE READS
spark impact in just one hour

IGNITE READS IS A NEW SERIES OF 1-HOUR READS WRITTEN BY WORLD-RENOWNED EXPERTS!

These captivating books will help you become the best version of yourself, allowing for new opportunities in your personal and professional life. Accelerate your career and expand your knowledge with these powerful books written on today's hottest ideas.

TRENDING BUSINESS AND PERSONAL GROWTH TOPICS

Read in an hour or less

Leading experts and authors

Bold design and captivating content